LOUISVILLE'S SOUTHERN EXPOSITION 1883-1887

The Board of Directors of
The Southern Exposition at Louisville, Ky.
requests the honor of the presence of
Mr William Alvord.
at the
Opening Ceremonies,
on Wednesday, August first, 1883.

Tiffany & Co. N.Y.

An invitation for the opening ceremonies for the Southern Exposition 1883. *Courtesy of Ken Maguire and the author.*

LOUISVILLE'S SOUTHERN EXPOSITION

1883–1887 THE CITY *of* PROGRESS

BRYAN S. BUSH

THE History PRESS

Published by The History Press
Charleston, SC 29403
www.historypress.net

Front cover image: Courtesy of *Harper's Weekly*.
Back cover images: Courtesy of James Calvert and the author.

First published 2011

Manufactured in the United States

ISBN 978.1.60949.143.7

Library of Congress Cataloging-in-Publication Data

Bush, Bryan S., 1966-
Louisville's Southern Exposition, 1883-1887 : the City of Progress / Bryan S. Bush.
p. cm.
Includes bibliographical references and index.
ISBN 978-1-60949-143-7
1. Southern Exposition (Louisville, Ky.) I. Title.
T705 1883 .B1 B87 2011
907.4'76944--dc22
2010050618

Special thanks must go to Ken Maguire, Margaret Young of the Conrad-Caldwell House, Marianna Zucker of the Brennan House, Ken and Peggy Kirkman, James Calvert and the Louisville Free Public Library.

Contents

Preface

Southern Exposition: 1883-1887

Before the Civil War, Louisville manufactured and supported not only agricultural products but also industrial products. Louisville had ties not only to the south but also the north. After the Civil War, Louisville, Kentucky, identified its city as being part of the south. One of the main reasons why the city identified with the south was because of the harsh treatment by the Union military leaders, such as Union generals Jeremiah Boyle and Stephen Gano Burbridge. By 1864, Louisville turned from its support of the Union and the Republican Party to supporting the Democrats and ex-Confederates. Many of Kentucky's political and civic leaders after the Civil War were ex-Confederate soldiers. The Southern Exposition's original idea was to showcase cotton "from seed to loom" and other agricultural products, but other earlier expositions already showcased cotton. Henry Watterson, the founder of the Southern Exposition, decided to change the focus of the exposition and showcase the new technology of the north. As an entrepreneur, the exposition constantly changed its displays and themes during the five-year run. For example, in 1884, the exposition changed to a military theme; in 1885, it was a world's fair, with exhibits from Mexico, Switzerland, France and many other countries; by 1886, the Southern Exposition featured dinosaurs; and when the exposition finally closed its doors in 1887, it focused on children's entertainment.

Although the exposition's original purpose was to "advance the material welfare of the producing classes of the South and West" and make money for local producers and merchants, the show accomplished many different firsts for Louisville and the country. The Southern Exposition had the largest bicycle track in the United States, the largest stockyards exhibit, the largest gathering of agricultural implements in the United States, the largest fireworks spectator area and the largest single contract for the incandescent light bulb. But the exposition also exposed many Louisville residents to operas and orchestras, which sparked a boom in the support of the arts after it closed. The exposition also sparked a housing boom in 1885, with houses built around it, which cost $6,000 in 1885 (a staggering $1.5 million today). After the doors closed, the exposition gave to an even larger housing boom with the construction of $10 million worth of homes in the area that was once the Southern Exposition grounds. The housing boom on the grounds led to the present-day St. James and Belgravia Court areas, with the nation's largest remaining collection of Edwardian and Romanesque homes in America.

The exposition may have tried to convey to the world that the show would showcase the south, but it became much more than that; it blended agriculture with modern technology, which fit more traditionally with Louisville's link with not only the south but also with the north.

Chapter 1
The History of Expositions and Fairs in the United States and Louisville

The history of expositions and fairs dates back as early as 1853, when New York held a world's fair. The city gave a lease of Reservoir Square for five years, rent free, but under the condition that the building would be constructed of glass and iron and the admission to the fair to be $0.50. Congress also passed an act constituting the building as a bonded warehouse, where foreign goods would not be charged an import tax. The building was in the form of a Greek cross, 865 feet long each way and 150 feet wide, with a central dome 125 feet high and 100 feet in diameter. And on one side, another building, 450 feet long and 75 feet wide, was erected for machinery. On July 14, President Franklin Pierce opened the exhibition, which lasted for 119 days. There were 4,800 exhibitors, with over half the fair's visitors being foreigners. The principal purpose of the exhibition was to showcase American machinery and agricultural implements. The cost of the building was $549,000, with the furnishings and fittings costing $100,000 dollars. Receipts from the sale of tickets and catalogues came to $840,000.[1]

In 1854, the show reopened with an additional $200,000, which exhausted the capital stock and two loans. Later, the building was loaned to the American Institute and used for annual fairs; but on October 15, 1858, the building burned to the ground, with all the contents.[2]

As the first American centennial approached, Philadelphia decided to put together a committee for a centennial fair. In March 1871, Congress passed a bill that became the basis to form a commission for the centennial. The following year, a commission was constituted, according to the congressional bill. On March 4, 1872, the commission met in Philadelphia. The expenses for the centennial would amount to $8,500,000, and in order to raise this money, Congress authorized a board of finance. The financial committee sold stock, with shares of $10 each. The committee raised $2,500,000. Congress gave $1,500,000, and other states gave the rest of the money. The president announced that the United States would celebrate the centennial, and the nations of the world were invited to participate. The city gave Fairmount Park to the commission. The following year, the foundation of Memorial Hall was laid with appropriate ceremonies. In September, work began on the main building and continued until February 1876. Machinery Hall was built between January and October 1875. The Horticultural Hall, the Agricultural Hall, the Government Building, the Women's Pavilion and structures belonging to states and foreign countries were also erected for the centennial. The largest of the buildings was the main building, which was being built in the form of a parallelogram, with a length of 1,880 feet and 464 feet in width. The building was made of glass and iron. The Art Gallery cost $1,500,000. The building was designed to be a permanent fixture.

On January 5, 1876, the exposition began to accept exhibits. On May 10, 1876, it opened with visitors attending from all over the world. The president, members of the Supreme Court, Congress, the diplomatic corps, the cabinet and many state and municipal officers declared the exposition open. President Ulysses S. Grant, with the emperor of Brazil at his side, opened the valves of the Cerliss engine. The wheels started, and the exposition was inaugurated. On November 10, 1876, Grant shut off the Cerliss engine, and the exposition came to an end.[3]

In 1881, Atlanta, Georgia, held the next exposition: the International Cotton Exposition. On October 5, 1881, Governor Alfred H. Colquitt opened the exposition; it closed on December 31, 1881. The main building was in the form of a cross, and plans included a cotton mill. The building was constructed of heavy timber. The building was 720 feet long and 400 feet wide. There was also the Agricultural Annex,

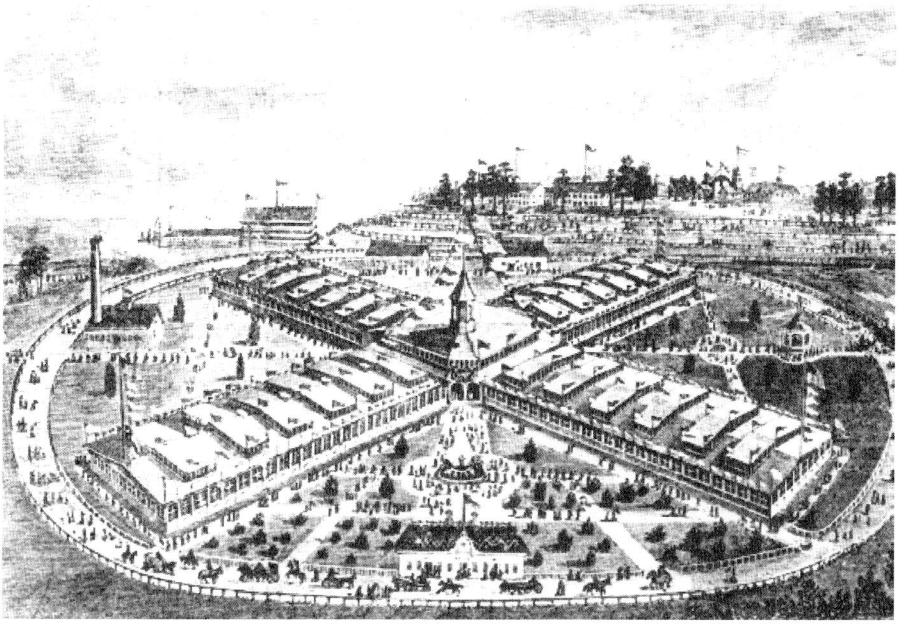

The Cotton Exposition of 1881 in Atlanta, Georgia. *Courtesy of the Atlanta History Center Archives.*

which was 275 feet by 100 feet, in which agricultural implements and machinery were displayed. The Carriage Annex was 210 feet by 100 feet, and it displayed carriages. Two buildings were set aside for minerals and woods, with the dimensions of the building 200 feet by 100 feet by 150 feet. There was also the Art and Industrial Hall, which was devoted to the exhibits of works of art and manufactured goods. There was the Judge's Hall, which could seat up to one thousand people and was also used for the judges to meet and for the various conventions and societies. The buildings covered 21 acres. Outside the buildings were plats of land where seeds were planted so the public could see cotton plants in every stage of culture and could judge the values of the various modes and systems of tillage. There were over 1,800 exhibits, of which the goods were American made. Prominence was given to cotton and everything related to the industry, but all other branches of industry were also on display. The cost of the building was $260,000, and with receipts and sale of the building to a stockyard company for $25,000 after the show closed, the revenue came to $280,000.[4]

EXPOSITIONS IN LOUISVILLE

On March 8, 1853, several Louisville citizens met for the purpose of forming an association in the mechanical arts. The organization was called the Kentucky Mechanics Institute; William Gallagher was the first president of the organization. The purpose of the institute was to hold an exposition on the mechanical arts. Once the money had been raised, the institute selected the upper floor of the Farmer's Tobacco warehouse, on the northeast corner of Second and Washington Streets, for the first exhibition. On October 11, 1853, the first Louisville exhibition opened to the public. The general public called the Mechanics Exposition a Mechanics Fair. On October 31, 1853, the exhibition came to a close. Over 250 diplomas were awarded. The exhibits had been rotated on a daily basis.[5]

With the success of the first exhibition, the Kentucky Mechanics Institute applied to the Kentucky legislature for a charter so the exhibition could become a permanent institution. On March 8, 1854, the legislature passed an act incorporating the exhibition with the officers and directors of the Kentucky Mechanics Institute. The owner of the warehouse did not want the exhibition to be held on his grounds, so the institute had to find a new location. The grounds located on the northwest corner of Walnut and Second Streets were leased, and a wooden building was designed by Stancliff and Vogdes. The project cost $4,000. On September 26, 1854, the exhibition opened to the public, with an inaugural address given by General William Preston. The exhibition closed its doors on November 18, 1854.

In the fall of 1855, the third exhibition was held in Louisville, and the members of the mechanics institute wanted to make the location at Walnut and Second Streets their permanent location. But the owner wanted to sell, and the institute did not want to buy the land, so in 1856, the institute moved to the northeast corner of Fourth and Broadway.

On September 30, 1856, William Atwood gave the inaugural address, and on October 29, 1856, the exhibition came to an end. Annual exhibitions were held each autumn until 1860. Before arrangements could be made for the next exhibition, the Civil War brought the exhibition to a halt. The Kentucky Mechanics Institute put on annual exhibitions from 1853 to 1860. In 1854, the institute acquired the six thousand volumes from the Mercantile Library Association and donated the library to the city of Louisville, which later changed the name to the Louisville Library. When the Civil War broke out, the books were put in boxes and stored for safekeeping in the city school at the corner of Fifth and Walnut Streets. Unfortunately, the Union soldiers found the boxes, broke them open and used the books for waste paper or for kindling to start fires. What was left of the collection went to the city and was placed in the care of the Young Men's Christian Association; the group later donated them to the Public Library of Kentucky, which ended up later at the Polytechnic Institute.[6]

The Civil War ended the mechanics institute, but by 1870, John T. Moore, Biderman DuPont, J.M. Robinson, N. Bloom, M. Muldoon and C.G. Jones went to the Jefferson County Court and filed for the articles of incorporation, under the name of the Louisville Industrial Exhibition. John Moore became president. In May 1872, the committee purchased a plot of land at the northeast corner of Fourth and Chestnut Streets for $96,500. The architects of Struby and Mergell designed the building. The stock sale raised $140,000, and a contract was made with Fitchner & Hale to erect the building. By August 2, work began on the brick building.

A stereograph card of the stoves display at the Louisville Industrial Exposition of 1872. *Courtesy of the Robert N. Dennis Collection of Stereographic Views, New York Public Library.*

A stereograph card of the lamps display at the Louisville Industrial Exposition of 1872. *Courtesy of the Robert N. Dennis Collection of Stereographic Views, New York Public Library.*

An interior view stereograph card of the Louisville Industrial Exposition of 1872. *Courtesy of the Robert N. Dennis Collection of Stereographic Views, New York Public Library.*

The Louisville Industrial Exposition. *Courtesy of the Prints and Photographs Division, Library of Congress.*

On July 28, 1872, the contractors completed the building. The building was 889 feet long, 250 feet wide and 2 stories high. On September 3, 1872, the exhibition opened to the public. Between six to ten thousand citizens attended the opening. Elisha Applegate was the person of honor, since she was born in Sullivan's Fort on the Beargrass Creek in 1782. Speeches were given by future governor Thomas Bramlette, General John W. Finnell and the Honorable Benjamin Webb.[7]

The cost of the building came to $100,000. The committee decided to have the first exhibition on the first Tuesday in September. On September 3, 1872, the Louisville Industrial Exhibition opened and continued until 1882. There was only one year where the exhibition not held, which was 1876, because the centennial was held in Philadelphia. At the Centennial Exposition, the displays included mechanical and industrial arts, including arts, natural history, geology, paintings and sculptures. The grounds and building cost $915,000. After the exhibition was over in 1882, the grounds were sold to the United States for a customhouse for $140,000, and the building and machinery sold for $13,000.

Chapter 2
The Idea and Building of the Southern Exposition

By 1880, Louisville was ready to hold another exposition, except on a larger scale. Louisville's residents had every reason to show to the country and world that their city had become a viable part of the commercial and agricultural world; it had become the largest tobacco market in the world. In 1861, Louisville produced 161,289 hogshead of tobacco, but by 1881, the city produced 571,949 hogshead. The district produced over twenty million gallons of whiskey every year and stood tenth in the nation for clearinghouses and ninth as a Federal collection district. Louisville produced more leather than any other city in America.[8]

The idea of holding the Southern Exposition in Louisville can be traced to letter published in the *New York Herald* in July 1880, written by Edward Atkinson of Boston. Atkinson's idea was for a grand exposition of cotton as the staple of the south, showing the product in all its stages, from seed to the different forms of manufacturing and the process of manufacturing of the cotton in all its forms, uses and ornamentation. Henry Watterson, chief editor of the *Louisville Courier-Journal*, supported the interests of Louisville and the south and decided to adopt Atkinson's idea.

Henry Watterson was a powerful voice in Louisville business and politics, using the paper as an instrument to wield his views. His early career was interesting, to say the least. He was born in Washington,

D.C., on February 16, 1840. He spent his days in Washington and Maury County, Tennessee, since his father was a representative for the Ninth Congressional District of Tennessee as a Democrat. After 1843, his father, Harvey, became editor for the *Washington Union*. In 1852, Watterson enrolled in the Academy of the Protestant Episcopal Church in Philadelphia. After graduation, he returned to McMinnville, Tennessee, to live with his parents.[9]

When the Civil War broke out, Watterson tried to avoid the war, but on a trip to Nashville to seek a position in a newspaper, he joined the Confederacy. Initially, he served on Confederate general Leonidas Polk's staff during his occupation of Columbus, Kentucky, but returned home because of an illness. After he recovered, he joined Confederate general Nathan Bedford Forrest's cavalry and participated in several raids.[10]

In 1862, Watterson quit the army and published a paper called the *Rebel* in Chattanooga, Tennessee. Watterson was highly critical of Confederate general Braxton Bragg. The *Rebel* became a favorite among Bragg's soldiers.[11]

When Union forces occupied Chattanooga, Watterson returned to Polk's staff and later transferred to Confederate general John Bell Hood's staff. Watterson eventually left Hood's staff and became editor for the *Montgomery Mail*. Before the war ended, Watterson moved to Cincinnati, Ohio, and became editor for the *Evening Times*.[12]

When the war ended, Watterson returned to Nashville to edit the *Republican Banner*. In 1868, Isham Henderson invited Watterson to Louisville to take over the *Louisville Journal* from current chief editor George W. Prentice. In October 1868, Watterson approached Walter Haldeman, chief editor of the *Louisville Courier*, about purchasing the *Journal*. Haldeman agreed and bought the *Journal*, along with the John Harney's *Democrat*. On November 8, 1868, the combination of the three newspapers became known as the *Louisville Courier-Journal*.[13] Even though Watterson served as editor of the *Courier-Journal*, he also served in the U.S. Congress, being elected in 1876. Watterson became the central figure in encouraging the Southern Exposition.

On August 20, 1880, Henry Watterson and the *Courier-Journal* published an editorial reviewing Atkinson's letter and supporting the idea of a Southern Exposition in Louisville. The central exhibit would be cotton. The paper called for the Louisville Board of Trade to take on the idea of an exposition.

A meeting was held the next day at the Louisville Board of Trade in order to discuss the idea. A committee of twelve was appointed to look into the matter and decide whether an exhibition was practicable. The committee reported to the board of trade on August 25 that the exposition would cost in excess of $200,000. The board of trade reported that they needed more time to study if Louisville was ready for an exposition. While Louisville mulled their decision, Atlanta, Georgia, beat Louisville to the draw and held their own Cotton Exposition. Louisville lost the chance "to become a city of the South."

The *Courier-Journal*'s idea was to have an exhibition of all the state's resources, agricultural, mineral and mechanical, in which cotton would take center stage, because cotton was a southern product and a staple of the south. The opinion of the people of Louisville was that the city of Louisville should continue what Atlanta started with their Atlanta Cotton Exhibition.

In December 1881, Henry Watterson again put forth an idea for an exposition. In October 1882, a committee formed to discuss the idea of an exposition with the streetcar lines, railroad officials and proprietors of hotels. On October 18, 1882, the committee reported that the public supported the idea. The committee recommended the formation of a stock company with a capital of $250,000 and planned to elect twenty-five men to sit on the board of directors. On October 25, 1882, the committee drafted the form of incorporation to raise a capital stock of $300,000, with the privilege to raise $500,000. The committee agreed to expand the board to fifty members, becoming known as the "Committee of Fifty." It was comprised of some of Louisville's most influential men, including S.L. Avery, Merriwether Lewis Clark Jr., Charles Ballard, R.W. Knott, W. Snead, George H. Hall, N. Bloom, St. John Boyle, Andrew Cowan, Henry Payne, H.A. Witherspoon, Andrew Buchanan, Bidermann DuPont, W.R. Belnap and Bennett Young.[14]

On October 27, the articles of incorporation named the exhibition: the Southern Exhibition at Louisville. The Committee of Fifty decided that the purpose of the exhibition should be:

> *to advance the material welfare of the producing classes of the South and West, to exhibit the products and resources of the Southern states to Northern and Eastern manufacturers and the implements and machines of the great industries of the former. But while the Exposition tends to embrace in its Southern exhibits all departments of Southern agriculture, forestry, mining, and commerce, special attention, prominence and consideration is given to cotton and its products, from "Seed to Loom!"*[15]

The Committee of Fifty appointed J.H. Lindenberger as chairman of the Finance Committee and John E. Green as second vice-president and chairman of the Committee on Buildings and Grounds. R.W. Knott was made chairman of the Committee on Advertising and Printing. The committee placed the opening of the exhibition on August 1, 1883, with it running for one hundred days. The committee made an offer for Mr. A. Bidermann DuPont's land near Central Park as the location of the exposition. Antoine Bidermann DuPont was one of the more powerful industrialists in Louisville. He was born in Wilmington, Delaware, on October 13, 1837, and was the youngest son of Alfred Victor Philadelphe and Margaretta DuPont. In 1854, Bidermann wanted to make a career of his own and left Delaware for Louisville with his older brother, Alfred DuPont. Alfred and his cousin, Charles DuPont Jr., bought a paper mill located on Tenth and Monroe (Rowan) Streets, with offices and warehouses on Sixth between Main and Market Streets. The company specialized in the manufacture of newsprint to be sold in the west. In 1857, Bidermann became a partner when his cousin sold his interest in the company. The paper mill became very successful, and Bidermann became the president of the Central Coal and Iron Company, with offices in both central Kentucky and Louisville, and the Central Passenger Railway Company, which operated mule-drawn streetcars. In 1879, Bidermann reorganized the board of trade and was elected to the new board of directors. The organization later became known as the Louisville Area Chamber of Commerce.[16]

After buying the land from Bidermann DuPont, the committee chose the plans for the Southern Exposition building from Kenneth McDonald and Cornelius Curtain. The cost of the building was determined to be $167,000. The committee approved $227,000 for music, lights and machinery for the building. On January 29, 1883, the committee managed to raise only $288,000, so it held a massive fundraiser at the opera house in Louisville and invited the cities of New Albany and Jeffersonville, Indiana, to participate. The event was a huge success and raised the money needed to complete the project.[17]

On January 30, 1883, McDonald and Curtain began construction of the buildings. On March 15, 1883, lumber arrived for the carpentry work, and soon the electricians and plumbers started their work on the massive structure. The contractors removed 35,000 cubic yards of ground. The first contract called for 4,000,000 feet of lumber, but an additional 650,000 feet of lumber would be necessary for the additional buildings. Over thirty-five thousand panes of glass were used in the construction of the building, along with twenty-five tons of white lead. Six thousand squares of shingles were used on the roof. The main building covered ten acres and was 600 feet wide and 900 feet long. Situated from the outer boundaries of the building were open courts, four in number, that were 945 feet by 100 feet in size. The cross-shaped figure left in the center of the structure was higher than the remainder of the building, which had an outside boundary that would be used as a promenade. The central pavilion was 100 feet square, and the corner pavilions were each 90 feet square. The curtains connecting the pavilion north and south were each

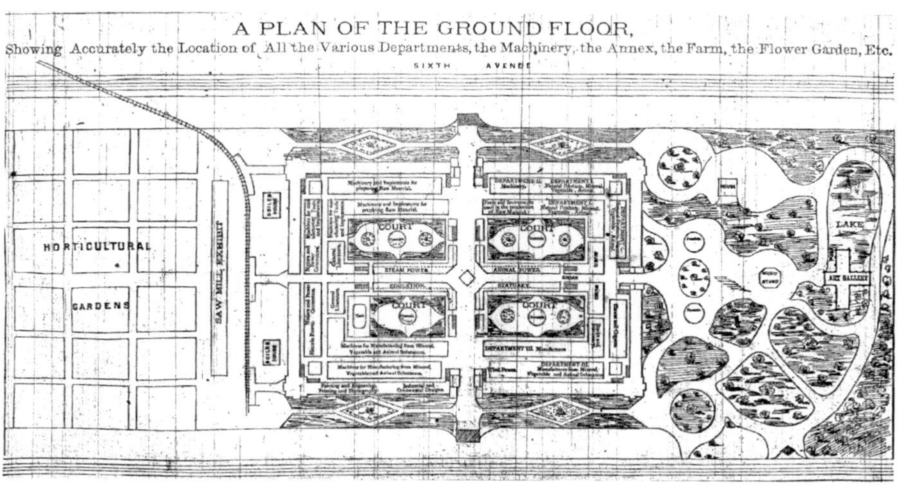

Ground plans for the Southern Exposition. *Courtesy of the* Louisville Courier-Journal.

The Southern Exposition building and surrounding grounds, *Harper's Weekly. Courtesy of the Ken Maguire collection.*

810 feet long, and those connecting east and west were 160 feet long. The central cross was 400 feet by 600 feet and was 110 feet wide and 45 feet high up to the bottom of the trusses. About 25 feet above the first floor, there were 5,000 feet of galleries extending around the building.[18]

The interior of the building had five departments for the exhibits. The northwest wing had natural products, such as mineral, vegetable and animal. The second department was devoted to machinery, occupied the southern area of the building and was comprised of tools and implements, motors and power generators, machinery and implements for preparing raw material, machines for manufacturing and machines for manufacturing tools and implements. The third department, which occupied the northwest area of the building, was devoted to manufactured products and included mineral, vegetable and animal substances. The fourth department concentrated on transportation and was located in the space between the north and northwest wings of the building, connecting the building north and south. The exhibit was devoted to animal, wind, steam and electrical power. The fifth department was devoted to music, literature and art and occupied the area running the dividing wings north and south; the area was comprised of piano, organs and other musical instruments, books and stationery, education, general literature, statuary, paintings and engravings, industrial and ornamental designs and scientific instruments and models.[19]

There were 3,700 feet of continuous skylights. At night, the entire building and annexes were lit with 4,600 incandescent light bulbs, provided by Thomas Edison's company; at that time, the arrangement was the largest contract made for lighting a building. In order to string the lights, it took one hundred men a month to complete the task, at a cost of $100,000, which included the price of the generators that supplied the lights with energy, which was provided by four of the Arlington & Sims engines and one large Reynolds Corliss engine. The Jenny Arc Light Company of Fort Wayne, Indiana, provided an additional seventy-five arc lights of two thousand candlepower each. The engines also provided electricity for an electric railway that was built to carry passengers on a narrow track that circled Central Park and passed through an artificial tunnel lighted by incandescent bulbs.[20]

The exposition grounds covered forty-five acres, which contained forests and flowerbeds. The park covered eighteen acres. The exposition ran just south of Central Park, from Fourth to Sixth Street and from Weissinger (now Park) Avenue to Hill Street. The 205-foot by 82-foot

The electric railway, which ran the perimeter of the Southern Exposition grounds, *Harper's Weekly*. *Courtesy of the Ken Maguire Collection.*

A view of Central Park, looking toward the front entrance of the Southern Exposition. *Courtesy of the Prints and Photographs Division, Library of Congress.*

A *Harper's Weekly* sketch of the Model Farm at the Southern Exposition grounds. *Courtesy of the Ken Maguire Collection.*

Right: A sketch of the Art Gallery. *Courtesy of the* Louisville Courier-Journal.

Below: The Southern Exposition Art Gallery, located in Central Park. *Courtesy of the* Louisville Courier Journal.

A sketch of the Music Hall at the Southern Exposition. *Courtesy of the* Louisville Courier-Journal.

by 50-foot arched hall with a skylight access art gallery was built on the northeast section of the park and had a fountain in the center, directly opposite from the 20-foot-wide archway entrance. The exposition also boasted a three-thousand-seat Music Hall, located in the center of the park. South of the main building and east of the sawmill annex was the field agricultural exhibit, which grew every staple vegetable of the south. The field comprised about ten acres and represented a southern plantation.

The Central Passenger Railway on Fourth Street approached the exposition from downtown Louisville, and the tracks ran right up to the door of the gatehouse at the eastern entrance. In a similar manner, the tracks approached on Sixth Street by the City Passenger Railway Company, which let off passengers at the door of the gatehouse on the western entrance. The north and south entrances were built to accommodate carriages. At each entrance of the gatehouses, there

A sketch of the interior of the Southern Exposition. *Courtesy of* Harper's Weekly.

A sketch of the front entrance to the Southern Exposition. *Courtesy of the* Louisville Courier-Journal.

were cloakrooms where visitors could leave their wraps. There were also restaurants and refreshment stands. The Louisville and Nashville Railroad extended their main line with a switch running north through Sixth Street, so that all visitors and freight could literally be brought to the doors of the exhibition, without even using a carriage, wagon or omnibus.[21]

Chapter 3

The Opening of the Southern Exposition

A President Comes to Visit

By the end of July 1883, the Southern Exposition, the Art Gallery and Central Park were ready for the public. To celebrate the grand opening, the citizens of Louisville draped every street and every building from downtown to the suburbs in holiday garments. Silk banners, streamers and pennants waved in the breeze or drooped from their staves. Visitors could look down any direction and see the kaleidoscope of colors. The citizens also hung small flags out every window, and the larger flags floated from the housetops or hung over the street from the third stories. The citizens draped the national colors on every column. Buntings and flags arranged on every device and variety hung on businesses on Main Street. On Eighth Street, decorations hung on every building. Market Street almost rivaled Main Street in the amount of decorations. Private residences and businesses on Fourth Street also decorated for the exposition. The Oak Hall Clothing Store, which was on the corner of Fourth and Jefferson, hung expensive bunting flags of all the nations on its building from the ground to the flagstaff, which flew the stars and stripes. An oil painting of President Chester Arthur hung on the Jefferson Street side of the building. All of the city buildings, including city hall, were decorated for the opening of the exposition and the arrival of special guests.

SECOND PART, Double Number

The Courier-Journal.

SECOND PART, Double Number

VOLUME LXV. NEW SERIES, NO. 5,328

THE GREAT SOUTHERN EXPOSITION!

THROWS ITS DOORS OPEN TO THE WORLD.

A VIEW OF THE MAGNIFICENT BUILDING.

Above: The August 1, 1883 front page of the *Louisville Courier-Journal*. *Courtesy of the* Louisville Courier-Journal.

Left: President Chester Arthur. *Courtesy of the Library of Congress.*

On a special train from Washington, D.C., President Chester Arthur and his party headed for Kentucky. The train traveled from White Sulphur to Mount Sterling, Kentucky, where the train stopped and the president made a speech to the citizens gathered at the station. After greeting the crowd, the train steamed off for Lexington. Thousands gathered at the station in Lexington. Senator James B. Beck and General Preston found their way through the crowd and took the president to the Phoenix Hotel. Waiting for the president at the hotel was the Lexington Committee. The committee took the president to Ashland, which was the former home of the great Kentucky senator, Henry Clay. After a tour of Clay's home, the party drove the president to a Kentucky horse farm owned by B.J. Treasy. Once the president observed the fine Kentucky-bred horses, they returned to the hotel, where he met the Louisville Committee, headed by Kentucky governor Luke P. Blackburn and Louisville mayor Charles D. Jacob. The other members of the committee who greeted the president were Judge Barr, former Confederate general Basil Duke, Major Speed, Mr. Bohne, General Elkin, Henry Watterson, D.W.C. Rowland, the Honorable Albert S. Willis and the Honorable Isaac P. Caldwell.[22]

The train was comprised of one engine, a coal car, four private cars and one parlor car. The estimated cost of the entire train was $200,000. As the train left the station, the company of Legross & Sutton decorated the engine with flowers, which were twined with floral wreaths.[23]

On July 31, 1883, a large crowd of ten thousand people assembled around the Short Line Railroad to greet President Chester Arthur and his entourage. General Taylor, the chief of police, with thirty-two policemen, managed to keep the platform at the depot and both sides of the track clear, so that the president and his party could make their way to their carriages. The citizens of Louisville also decorated the depot with tri-colors, with the roof and corners all draped in bunting and festoons, while thousands of flags—both large and small—hung from every hook. Ten carriages lined up to take the president and his staff to the Galt House. Bly's Artillery, stationed east of First Street, fired a salute upon the arrival of the train. The president brought with him Secretary Folger; General Preston; Judge Barr; Postmaster General Walter Q. Gresham; Mayor Charles Jacob; Secretary Robert Lincoln, Abraham Lincoln's son; Governor Blackburn; and Senator Bayard, along with many others. The

Advertising souvenir card from the 1883 Southern Exposition for J.B. Wilder, a local wholesale pharmacist from Louisville, Kentucky. *Courtesy of the author.*

line of carriages, with the president's carriage leading, rode to Second Street and then up Main to the Galt House, followed by the rushing, cheering crowd.

Another committee, made up of the members of Grand Army of the Republic (GAR) posts at Jeffersonville and Louisville, awaited another train from Chicago. The Grand Army of the Republic was comprised of former Union soldiers who fought during the Civil War. A special train carried Union general Phil Sheridan, who was a cavalry commander during the Civil War. Once the train arrived, the committee members' Grand Army of the Republic railway car was hitched to General Sheridan's train, and the special train then headed for Louisville. Once there, the rear door of the car was opened, and Colonel Bennett Young walked out, followed by General Sheridan. The committee, headed by Colonel George Northup, pressed forward and shook hands with General Sheridan. Afterward, the rest of the committee of about thirty men greeted Sheridan. General Sheridan commented to the *Courier-Journal* that he had not been in the city for thirteen years, or since the reunion of the Union Army of Tennessee, and that Louisville had become an important city. His most distinct remembrance of the city was connected to when he had to erect fortifications around the city during the Civil War. General Sheridan had traveled from Chicago with his wife and brother; Michael Sheridan; General J. Tompkins; Colonel G.C. Wharton; Colonel F.K. Faulkner; R.M. Kelley, president of the GAR post at Louisville; and Colonel Bennett Young. Sheridan and his staff stayed at the Galt House.[24]

When Sheridan and his party arrived at the Galt House, they were met by another welcoming committee, headed by Colonel Buckner, Mr. Pettitt and others, who accompanied them to their parlors.

At the entrance to the hotel the general reception committee—comprised of Bidermann DuPont, president of the Southern Exposition; Dr. L.P. Yandell; Dr. George W. Griffiths; Judge T.L. Burnett; M.A. Smith; the Honorable Lafferty Joseph; George Buchanan; Theodore Swartz; James Lithgow; George Morris; William Cornwall Sr.; James Trabue; S.B. Churchill; Colonel J.F. Buckner; Cuthbert Bullitt; C.E. Sears; George W. Armstrong; John Carter; William Krippenstaple; Colonel Auxier; R.A. Robinson; Confederate general Simeon Bolivar Buckner; J.M. Robinson; N. Bloom; Dr. T.S. Bell; and Henry Watterson—greeted the president, General Sheridan and their parties. Once everyone had been introduced, the president and General Sheridan, the committee, the president's and General Sheridan's parties sat down for a dinner. After the dinner, the president and his party were taken to the palatial residence of Mr. F.D. Carley, where a reception was given with refreshments. After the reception, the carriages took the president and his party back to the Galt House.[25]

On August 2, 1883, soon after breakfast, the citizens of Louisville crowded around the Galt House to the Southern Exposition. By 11:00 a.m. on August 2, 1883, the early morning trains brought enough visitors to where they crowded Main Street, from Brook to Sixth Street, and areas leading to Central Park, where people wore their best attire and were anxious to greet the distinguished visitors at the gates to the Exposition. The citizens of Louisville made sure that every column on Fourth Street was decorated in red, white and blue. Standing on the corner of Market Street, a visitor could see flags, bunting, Chinese lanterns, evergreen wreaths, arches, pictures and festoons that looked very much oriental in nature. City hall had flags, several miles of bunting and lines of Chinese lanterns as well. A large flag hung over the Masonic Temple. The Louisville and Nashville Railroad on the corner of Second and Main had their entire front covered in red, white and blue. The entrance to the building was covered in banners of silk, fringed with yellow flock. Banners wrapped around every column and swung their silken folds from every window. At the L&N office, on the corner of Fourth and Main, they hung a huge portrait of President Arthur, surrounded by large L&N signs in red paper.

At 11:00 a.m., General Taylor, chief of police, accompanied by a squad of policemen on foot and about fifty on horseback, drew up in front of the Galt House. Companies A, B, C, D and F of the Louisville Legion, under the command of Colonel John B. Castleman, Major J.H. Leathers and James Speed marched four rows deep from the armory of Seventh Street and down Main Street to martial music of the Legion band up the street; they ended at the Galt House. The Louisville Legion has a long and distinguished military heritage. Founded in 1836, Thomas Anderson organized a company of infantry known as the Louisville Guards. Three years later, in 1838, the Kentucky General Assembly chartered the Louisville Guards into a new organization called the Louisville Legion. By 1845, six companies of infantry drilled at the Oakland Racecourse on Seventh Street and marched in parades. In 1846, the Louisville Legion joined to fight the Mexican War. The Legion became known as the First Regiment of Foot, Kentucky Volunteers. Stephen Ormsby commanded the regiment and served under General Zachary Taylor's army in northern Mexico. After the Mexican War, the Louisville Legion consisted of several companies and was commanded by the most prominent citizens of Louisville.[26]

When the shots were fired in April 1861 on Fort Sumter in Charleston, South Carolina, Kentucky declared neutrality. President Lincoln gave Louisville native Lovell Rousseau, who was brigadier general of the Louisville Legion, permission to raise troops for the defense of the Union. Because of Kentucky's neutrality, Rousseau moved his regiment to Camp Joe Holt, in Jeffersonville, Indiana. Ten companies were raised, and the regiment was officially mustered into the Union army and designated the Fifth Kentucky Infantry, United States, with Rousseau as colonel. The regiment went on to fight at the

Battle of Shiloh, Stone's River and the Chattanooga Campaign, and it was involved in the march to Atlanta.[27]

After the Civil War, the Louisville Legion disbanded for ten years; but in 1878, the Legion reorganized as the First Regiment of Infantry, Kentucky State Guard, but was more commonly known as the Louisville Legion. The Legion had eight companies of infantry, one of which trained as an artillery company. The commander of the Louisville Legion was John B. Castleman.[28]

Castleman was born on June 30, 1841, in Lexington, Kentucky. He received his education at Fort Hill Academy in Lexington. He entered Transylvania University but left in 1861 to join the Confederacy. In 1862, Castleman, along with forty-two men he recruited, became part of Confederate general John Hunt Morgan's men. Castleman received the rank of captain and commanded Company D, Second Kentucky Cavalry. He eventually reached the rank of major. Castleman led an attempt in 1864 to free CSA prisoners at Camp Morton. With a band of guerillas, he left for St. Louis, hoping to burn Union supply boats at the wharf. Union forces captured Castleman at Sullivan, Indiana, in October 1864, and he was placed in federal prison in Indianapolis, Indiana, until the end of the war. He was exiled and then pardoned by President Andrew Johnson. After his pardon, he moved to Louisville in 1867 and received his law degree from the University of Louisville. He entered the insurance business with his father-in-law, John Barbee, establishing the firm Barbee & Castleman. In 1880, Castleman became colonel of the Louisville Legion. Just before the Southern Exposition opened to the public, Governor J. Proctor Knott appointed Castleman adjutant general.[29]

As the Legion approached the Galt House, a long line of carriages drew up in front of the hotel. President Arthur, Louisville mayor Charles Jacob and Charles Pettet entered the first carriage. At 1:00 p.m., the carriages arrived at the exposition building. In front of the main entrance to the exposition, the military drew up in line, and the band played "Hail Columbia." The police escort directed the carriages to a special entrance to the building. After President Arthur, along with Mayor Jacob and Charles Pettet and the rest of the party dismounted from their carriages, President Arthur and the rest of the party made their way to the hall and up into the stand, where thousands of shouting spectators greeted him.

The stand could fit up to 250 people. Flowers and banners covered the stand. The president and his party marched under an archway of rare tropical flowers and green plants. As the president approached the stage, walking down to the front of the stand arm in arm with Mr. Bidermann DuPont and Mayor Charles Jacob, the band played "Hail to the Chief." The stage held two large chairs, one for the president and the other for the governor. After the cheers for the president and his party subsided, the Reverend Dr. Perkins of St. Paul's Episcopal Church gave a prayer. At the end of the prayer, Mayor Charles D. Jacob greeted the president, and after a brief speech, he and the president shook hands. Governor Blackburn arose, took the president's arms and said: "Fellow citizens, it is my pleasure and I have the honor of introducing to you the Chief Executive of the United States, our President, Chester A. Arthur." The president stood and gave a small speech. At the end of the speech, Arthur declared: "I now declare that the Southern Exposition is open, and may

President Chester Arthur arriving at the Southern Exposition. *Courtesy of* Harper's Weekly, *1883.*

President Chester Arthur speaking to crowd. *Courtesy of* Harper's Weekly, *1883.*

God speed the fulfillment of all the lofty and ennobling purposes."[30] As President Arthur pulled the rope, setting the machinery in motion, bells rang, machinery clanged and prolonged shouts arose. There were frequent shouts for Robert Lincoln. Lincoln rose and bowed, but he did not address the crowd. The crowd called for General Phil Sheridan to speak, but he also sat in his chair and did not address the crowd. A choir of over 500 people, led by Director of the Oratorio Society Donald McPherson, along with the band and a massive grand organ, played and sang "My Country Tis of Thee"; next came Signor Cappa's selection, the overture of Weber. During the performance, Arthur and his party left the stand across the hall, passing around the great organ and out to the park. Next followed Handel's "See the Conquering Hero," "Star-Spangled Banner," "Way Down Upon Sewanee River," "Dixie" and, finally to close out the morning performance, "Awakening of the Line."

An escort of six policemen accompanied the president on his tour of the grounds. Arthur, along with Mayor Jacob and Bidermann DuPont, inspected the exposition. The party started at the north entrance and turned right, going through the east side of the building and reaching the south end, where the machinery was all in motion. The president stopped to look at the large Cerliss engine. The party continued on toward the west side of the building. Passing along the exhibits displayed, the party went directly to the north entrance and out across the park to the Art Gallery in Central Park. Arthur spent an hour looking at the four hundred or more paintings and stated that no collection excelled that in the Art Gallery. The Art Gallery contained private collections from J.P. Morgan; August Belmont; Jay Gould; Victor Newcomb, former president of the Louisville and Nashville Railroad; and John Jacob Astor. The Smithsonian Institute furnished paintings, and former president Ulysses Grant loaned a collection of curios, given to him during his travels around the world. Paul Phillipoteaux's ten- by twenty-foot painting of *The French Revolution of 1848* was the highlight of the collection. Robert Koehler and Thomas Eakins displayed their art. *A Gainesboro Landscape* and *Sunset* by George Inness were also on loan from other museums. While in the Art Gallery, Mayor Jacob introduced prominent citizens of Louisville to the president.[31]

At 2:00 p.m., Arthur headed to Mr. DuPont's house, near Central Park. After an hour luncheon, the president and his entourage headed back to

1883 Stereograph of the machinery exhibit at the Southern Exposition. *Courtesy of the Robert N. Dennis Collection of Stereographic Views, New York Public Library.*

the Galt House. When Arthur arrived at the Galt House, W.O. Dodd, Walter Halderman, John Kline, John Speed, James Beattie, F.D. Stone, John Mason Brown and Dr. Preston B. Scott presented to the president a Meek reel made of the finest workmanship. President Arthur was an avid angler, and the Louisville anglers' society presented the president with the reel. Mr. B.F. Meek personally made the reel, and George Wolf made the alligator-skin box, lined with velvet and silk.[32]

At 7:00 p.m., the presidential party entered their carriages at the private entrance of the Galt House, were driven from Third Street to Walnut Street and steered into the rooms of the Pendennis Club for dinner. The front of the building was decorated with flags and bunting and illuminated with hundreds of Chinese lanterns and transparencies. The eighty-foot table was loaded with delicacies. General Sheridan and his party did not attend the banquet because his party had already boarded the train and headed home.[33]

During the first night of the Southern Exposition, the streets were crowded with people and illuminated Chinese lanterns in every size. The lanterns hung from windows, verandas and branches of trees, or they extended from one roof to another. Most of the lanterns came from New

This and next two pages: A photograph from the Doerr Photographic Art Gallery, which was located on Twelfth and Market Streets, in Louisville, Kentucky. On the back of the photograph, it advertises that the gallery won awards at the Southern Exposition for best photography several years in a row. *Photograph courtesy of James Calvert.*

AWARDED TO
J. Henry Doerr
Louisville Ky.
1885

THE SOUTHERN EXPOSITION
LOUISVILLE KY. 1886

THE SOUTHERN EXPOSITION
LOUISVILLE KY. 1883
AWARDED TO
J. Henry Doerr
Louisville Ky.
1884
AWARDED TO
J. Henry Doerr
Louisville Ky.
1885
THE SOUTHERN EXPOSITION
LOUISVILLE KY. 1886
Doerr
12TH & Market Sts.
LOUISVILLE, KY.
Duplicates at any Time.

In the 1883 *Official Catalog of the Southern Exposition*, J. Henry Doerr is listed as a photographic exhibitor. *Courtesy of the University of Louisville Archives.*

York. The president and some of his party traveled around the city and stopped to witness some of the illuminated displays.[34]

By 8:30 p.m., over five thousand people gathered to see the exposition building and displays. People paid fifty cents to enter the exposition to see the 100 arch lights and the 1,800 incandescent lights, which lit up the building at night. According to legend or tradition, when Thomas Edison arrived at the Exposition Hall, he discovered that the power system had broken down. Since his company had supplied the power, he felt a responsibility to get the lights back into working order. He immediately went down to the Exposition Hall's lower floors and joined the workmen who were trying to put the generator back together. When he fixed the problem, Edison emerged back up to the Exposition Hall, but he was covered in grime; the crowd cheered anyway, and he joined the dinner reception at the Galt House and finished his dinner.[35]

Southern Exposition souvenir coin for 1883. *Courtesy of the Ken Maguire Collection.*

Under the incandescent lights, in the concert hall, people came to hear the largest grand organ in the southwest and the famous Seventh Regiment Band of New York, under the direction of Signor Cappa. Signor Cappa, leader of the Seventh Regiment Band, was born in 1834 in Alesandra, Italy. His father was a soldier of fortune and fought with Napoleon when he took on Russia. His father rose to the rank of major, but a bullet wound in his leg—received during the retreat from Moscow—was fatal. He died when Cappa was only four years old. Four years later, Cappa began to study music. Because his father had been a soldier, Cappa entered the Royal Academy at Austi. At the age of fifteen, Cappa enlisted in the army, becoming the trombonist for the Sixty Lancers. Six years later, he left the Lancers to enlist in the United States Navy and joined the crew of the U.S. frigate *Congress* at Geneva. Two years later, he landed in New York and became an American. When he landed in America, he spent seven years with Theodore Thomas, who, at that time, had the best orchestra in America. Cappa joined the Seventh Regiment Band and had already been a member of the band for over twenty-three years when he played at the exposition. He married and had seven children. Cappa became the best of the military musicians, and his band was considered, at the time, one of the finest regimental bands in America. The exposition spent $35,000 to bring Cappa's band to Louisville.

Spectators overflowed the lower floor and the galleries of the second story. The Seventh Regiment began the concert with the William Tell Overture, and then Mr. T. Currie played "My Old Kentucky Home" with a trombone solo. Mrs. S.J. Friedenheimer sang "Inflammatus," along with organ, large chorus and orchestra. The Seventh Regiment Band also played "Fantasie Militarie." The highlight of the evening was when the five-hundred-person chorus from Louisville sang Handel's "Hallelujah Chorus." The exposition spent $107,220 on musical entertainment. By 10:30 p.m., the exposition closed their doors for the day. Over twenty thousand people attended the first day.[36]

The back of an advertisement card for the McCormick Harvesting Machinery Company, 1883, from the Southern Exposition. *Courtesy of the Ken Maguire Collection.*

The front of the advertisement card for the McCormick Harvesting Machinery Company, 1883. *Courtesy of the Ken Maguire Collection.*

Back of the advertising card for the McCormick Harvesting Machinery Company, 1883. *Courtesy of the Ken Maguire Collection.*

The front of the advertising card for the McCormick Harvesting Machinery Company. *Courtesy of the Ken Maguire Collection.*

On August 2, at 8:00 a.m., President Chester Arthur and his party left Louisville on the Louisville–New Albany–Chicago line. During the previous day, the ferryboats made over two hundred trips to Louisville. The city's motto became Progress. Louisville bought over a quarter million flags for the opening event, five hundred policemen, watchmen and detectives were on duty and 1,300 carloads of people came on trains across the bridge from Indiana into Kentucky to witness the opening. One of the notable visitors who arrived for the exposition was Dr. Ed Richardson, the largest cotton planter in the world and the president of the World's Industrial and Cotton Centennial Exposition. Dr. William F. Taylor, president of the American Humane Society and the Nautical School and the founder of the floating hospital system for serving sick children arrived at the Galt House for the exposition.

The Tennessee state display at the exposition highlighted its tobacco industry. The exhibit showcased Tennessee's educational facilities such as Vanderbilt, Tennessee University, University of the South, Southwestern Baptist University, Southwestern University and Fisk University. The Tennessee exhibit pointed out that the state grew Irish potatoes, sweet potatoes, melons, pumpkins, squash, beans, peas, turnips, sorghum, peaches, apples, pears, plums, cherries, strawberries, blackberries, dewberries, raspberries, gooseberries, huckleberries and currants. It also highlighted its vast ore resources. The exhibit was comprised of a thirty-

Souvenir coin from the Southern Exposition with the motto Progress. The city of Louisville adopted the slogan City of Progress during the Southern Exposition. *Courtesy of Ken Kirkman.*

foot-high pyramidal octagon that was surrounded by arches, which were supported at each of the eight corners by two pillars of Tennessee's eight varieties of commercial wood. The bases of the pillars were decorated, each with a panel of like growth. Forty square outposts formed a quadrangle, forty-two by twenty-five feet apart, surrounding the interior

Back side of the souvenir coin from the Southern Exposition. The stamp date on the coin is 1885. *Courtesy of Ken Kirkman.*

A bronze plaque located on Main Street in front of the present-day Frazier International History Museum, which stated the city of Louisville's motto of Progress during the Southern Exposition. *Courtesy of the author.*

pillars and pyramid. The latter was shelved on four sides, and the shelves filled with specimens, geological and agricultural. Into each outside post and on each of the sides, a glass plate of equal length was fitted, protecting and displaying a variety of cereals. The roof was covered with shingles of bunting, made of miniature "stars and stripes." A collection of ores and copper, along with iron ore, oxides, carbonates, lead ore, lead and other products, were on display. They also had a display of Tennessee's variety of marbles. There was a display of building stones, whetstones, granites and sandstones. An immense block of Sewanee coal was on display, including a pyramid of coke. The exhibit had twenty-two varieties of Fults wheat, oats, barley and millet. Shelves contained potatoes, corn, ground peas, bluegrass, rope and cloth from the loom.

Another of the prominent displays at the Exposition belonged to the Bridesburg Manufacturing Company of Philadelphia, Pennsylvania. The company made machinery to process cotton and wool. The machinery of the company occupied a large space. The machine was the largest and most complete exhibit of textile fabric machinery ever put into operation by any firm in the world.

When the doors closed on November 1, 1883, over 30,000 people attended the exhibition that day alone. During the one hundred days the exposition ran, over 770,129 people attended the event, with an additional 200,933 admitted on passes.[37] To put the numbers into perspective, the amount of people who attended the exposition exceeded over six times the city population, which, at the time, was 123,762 people.

Chapter 4

The Southern Exposition Puts on a Military Show

The Southern Exposition of 1883 exceeded anyone's expectations. It was the most profitable exhibition ever held, and the exhibitors made money; for example, of the six hundred carloads of machinery from the eastern states, less than one hundred carloads went back to the states, because the articles on exhibit were sold during the exhibition. The show was a perfect combination of north and south; Northern manufacturers brought manufactured and manufacturing articles that met the needs of the southern market, and the southern market brought raw materials, such as cotton, coal, iron, trees and field products for the northern markets. The exhibitors that made money on the first exposition felt that the board of directors of the Southern Exposition should attempt a second year for the exposition. Before the doors closed on the first one, the board doubted that they had the authority to put on another exposition. They would have to ask the stockholders. The issue was about money and whether they could afford to hold another exposition. Some of the owners of the land on which part of the exposition sat refused to extend the lease of the property and wanted their property bought outright. The general manager and stockholders held a meeting and decided to reopen the show and raise $200,000 to buy the land.

A new organization followed with Bennett Young as president of the Southern Exposition; J.H. Lindenberger, vice-president; N. Bloom as

SOUTHERN EXPOSITION

AT LOUISVILLE, KY.

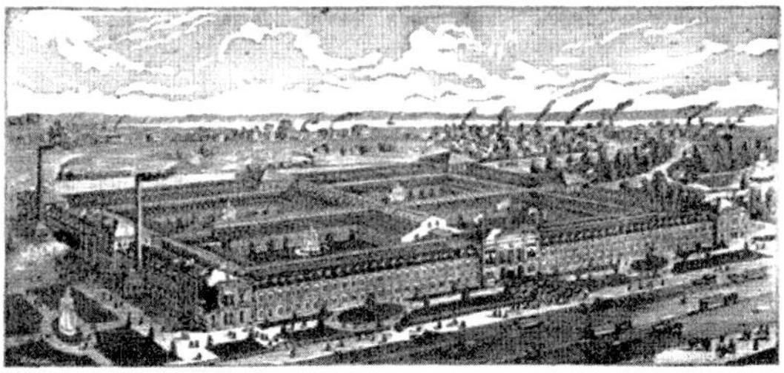

View of the Main Building, 920 x 630 Feet. Thirteen Acres under one roof.

Opens August 16, 1884, Closes October 25, 1884.

TO THE PUBLIC.

The undersigned have been named by the managers of the Southern Exposition as Commissioners for this county for the Exhibition of 1884.

State Appropriations.

The State of Kentucky has made an appropriation of $10,000 for the purpose of fostering and assisting the counties in making a favorable display of the resources of the State. This sum is placed under the control of a Commission, of which the State Geologist is Chairman, and a portion of it will undoubtedly be set apart for the benefit of this county.

Kentucky's Opportunity.

Kentucky, so great in her resources, has never had an opportunity like the present for demonstrating to the world the extent and richness of those resources, as this is the first organized effort ever made by the State at large to secure proper display of its immense capacities.

For the Whole People.

This opportunity is not for one section of the State, but for the whole people of Kentucky. It will present our State with all its wealth, resources, and attractions before the world, and will give each county its proper place in the grand aggregation. The county that most interests itself in the effort will make the best showing for its means and will be judged accordingly. It is, therefore, every one's interest to make the best display we can.

A Great Exposition.

The managers of the Southern Exposition have added new and wonderful attractions to the display this year, and every citizen of Kentucky will feel a just pride in the continued success of this, the largest Exposition ever successfully organized and maintained in this country, except the Centennial of 1876. It is estimated that the admissions of **Kentucky People** alone will number over **500,000,** and on the basis of last year's admissions and the new attractions that the general admissions will number **1,500,000.**

Our County.

Our county should make a creditable display. We have plenty of resources and with co-operation of all our people we can make a splendid exhibit. We ask suggestions and contributions from every spirited citizen of the county, and we hope this effort to advance the interests of the county and State will be heartily seconded by our people. For any special information write to Bennett H. Young, President, or J. M. Wright, General Manager, Southern Exposition, at Louisville, Ky., or apply to any of the Commissioners.

J. D. ELLIOTT, Bardstown, Ky.,
JNO. S. HUMPHREYS, " "
G. M. ABELL, Coxe's Creek, Ky.,
A. R. CAROTHERS, Bardstown, Ky.,
WM. SAMUELS, " "
JNO. A. FULTON, " "

COMMISSIONERS for County of NELSON.

Advertisement banner for the Southern Exposition, 1884. *Courtesy of the Library of Congress.*

A bird's-eye view by William F. Clarke of the Southern Exposition, 1883. *Courtesy of the Library of Congress.*

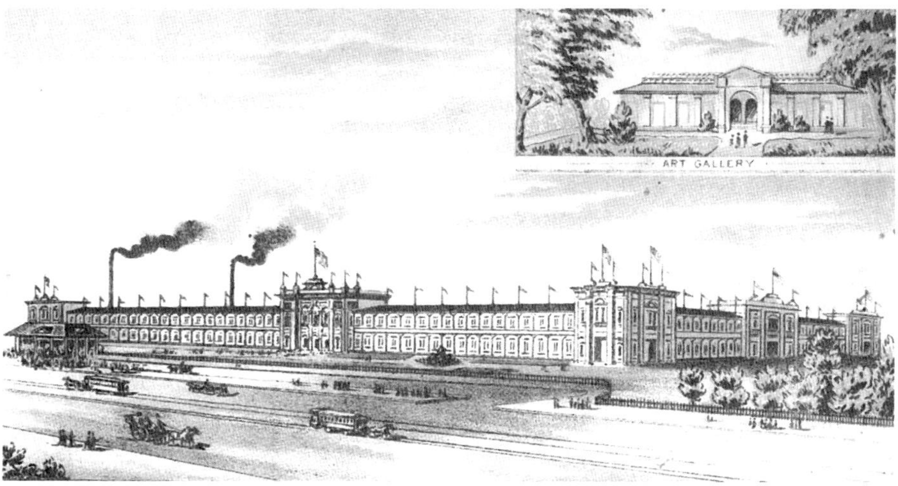

An 1884 advertising card for the Southern Exposition. *Courtesy of the author.*

second vice-president; John Green, third vice-president; J.W. Stine as fourth vice-president; Charles Pettet, fifth vice-president; J.M. Wright as general manager; J.H. Lindenburger as treasurer; and W.G. Colewey as secretary. Bennett Young was born on May 25, 1843, in Nicholasville,

Kentucky. Bennett's father, Robert, started a hat factory in Nicholasville, raising a small fortune, which he used to buy a two-story mansion and a plantation six miles west of Nicholasville. He attended Bethany Academy and, later, Centre College at Danville. In 1863, Bennett left Centre and enlisted in the Eighth Kentucky Cavalry, under the command of Confederate general John Hunt Morgan. In July 1863, Morgan made a daring raid through Kentucky, Indiana and Ohio, but on July 26, 1863, Morgan's luck ran out. Most of his command was captured at New Lisbon, Ohio, including Bennett Young and General Morgan, and some of his command, including Bennett Young, were placed in the Ohio State Penitentiary. Eventually Union authorities moved Bennett Young to Camp Douglas, near Chicago, Illinois. Young escaped the prison camp, and he was able to make his way to Canada. While in Canada, he enrolled at the University of Toronto, but in 1864, he left the college and managed to make his way back to the Confederate capital in Richmond, Virginia. He managed to secure the position of lieutenant and was given orders to harass Union troops behind enemy lines. He launched a raid against St. Albans, Vermont, robbing gold and currency for the Confederacy. He managed to make his way back to Canada. The United States asked for Canada to send him back to the United States for trial, but Young fled to Ireland. He studied at Queen's College, in Belfast, Ireland, and took courses at the University of Edinburgh, Scotland.[38]

In 1868, he returned to America and settled in Louisville, practicing as a lawyer. He became one of the city's most regarded trial attorneys. He reorganized the Louisville, New Albany, and Chicago Railroad and served as president from 1883 to 1884. From 1885 to 1886, he served as president of the Kentucky and Indiana Bridge Company. He also organized the Louisville Southern Railroad. He was also president of the Kentucky School for the Blind and was active in Confederate activities.[39]

The board of directors for the Southern Exposition consisted of Charles T. Ballard, St. John Boyle, John Mason Brown, Merriwether Lewis Clark Jr., W.A. Davis, George Gaulbert, J.J. Harbison, George Hull, Edward McKenna, J.M. Robinson, J.M. Wright, Charles Goldsmith, T.E.C. Brinly, W.W. Hite, Thomas Hays, Jesse Middleton, George Griffiths, John B. Castleman, Julius Winter, Temple Bodley, W.H. McKnight, H.P. Forwood and John Leathers.

The lineage of one of the board members, Merriwether Lewis Clark Jr., was an integral part of Louisville's history. He was born on January 27, 1846, in Louisville. He was the grandson of explorer and Missouri governor General William Clark, of the famous Lewis and Clark expedition. William Clark's brother, George Rogers Clark, founded Louisville and was a Revolutionary war hero. His grandfather on his paternal side of the family, Samuel Churchill, was one of the founders of the Oakland Racecourse at Seventh and Hill Streets. His father was Major Merriwether Lewis Clark Sr., who was aide-de-camp and in-law to General Stephen Watts Kearny of the Mexican War. His mother was Abigail Prather Churchill, who was one of the first founding families of Kentucky. Merriwether's father owned twenty-five horses. At the time, Merriwether Lewis Clark Jr. lived in St. Louis, Missouri.

In 1787, the Churchills moved to Louisville and bought three hundred acres of land. When Merriwether Lewis Clark Jr.'s mother died in 1852, he lived with his aunt and her sons, John and Henry Churchill. The Churchills loved horse racing. Merriwether attended St. Joseph's College in Bardstown, Kentucky, and upon graduation, he took a job as a teller at the Second National Bank in Louisville. After a few years, he changed jobs and entered the tobacco business. In 1872, a group of horse breeders approached Merriwether and asked if he would assist in resurrecting the horse-racing industry in Louisville. They knew of Merriwether Clark Jr.'s linage and thought he would be a good choice. In order to better understand the horse-racing industry, he visited England and France and brought back the idea of building a racetrack in Louisville. The Churchills leased the land for the racetrack and provided the financial backing. Merriwether became the president and on-site manager for Churchill Downs. In 1874, Merriwether founded the Louisville Jockey Club and Driving Park Association. On May 17, 1875, Churchill Downs opened for business, and the first Kentucky Derby was held. Ten thousand people attended the opening race, watching Aristides win. Clark spent most of his life promoting and operating the track.[40]

The board of directors made a big change as to the length of the exposition's run. No longer would it last for one hundred days. The exposition would open August 16 and close its doors on October 25. The exposition began to make improvements and expanded its displays.

Before the show opened, on the northern end of the building, its workmen were putting up the Hopkins County exhibit, which occupied thirty feet by forty-two feet and displayed coal, fruit and agricultural products. In the northeast corner court, exposition workers erected the frame of a house, measuring sixty feet by thirty feet, and on the frame were glazed transparent photographs on glass. The photographs showcased Kentucky views, such as bluegrass farmers and the mineral regions. The government furnished seventy-five pictures, with scenes of the far west and southwest. The interior of the framed house was used as a conservatory with a variety of plants.

The Louisville and Nashville Railroad exhibit stayed the same when the displays came to wood and the state's natural resources, but the exhibits on fruits and agricultural products were more elaborate and varied and the display of coal was expanded. On the machinery end of the building, space began to fill up, and several important displays made their appearance. A cotton gin and cotton compress were among the larger displays added to the exposition.

The exposition built a track and parade ground. In the center of the parade ground was an iron tower, which stood 125 feet high; the Jenny Arc Light Company built it. On top of the open iron tower were ten electric lights of two thousand candlepower each. On the Fourth Street line of cars, the workmen laid track so that the rail cars entered the Fourth Street entrance. Streetcars were now able to run up to the Fourth and Sixth Streets' entrances.

The exposition directors decided to not only expand the Kentucky exhibit, but they also added a livestock display, which was not featured in 1883. Kentucky exhibited sires, dams, running sires, cattle, sheep and hogs. The goal was to showcase Kentucky as a superior breeding place.

Another feature added to the exposition would be a "free for all" competitive drill (infantry only) that would take place on August 26, 27 and 28. The first prize was $3,000, second place was $1,000 and third place was $500. Officers from the United States Army determined the winners. The Kentucky State Guard supplied the tents and equipment, and arrangements were made for the troops to camp near the exposition grounds. The exposition gave free admission to all uniformed companies that came to visit. Cappa's Seventh Regiment Band provided the military music at dress parades and escorted the companies to and from their drill grounds. The companies that registered for the competition were the Centralia Light Guards of Centralia, Missouri; the Brookfield Rifles of Brookfield, Missouri; the Tredway Rifles (Reserves) of St. Louis, Missouri; the Quapaw Guards of Little Rock, Arkansas; the Porter Rifles of Nashville, Tennessee; the Indianapolis Light Infantry of Indianapolis, Indiana; and the Montgomery Grays of Montgomery, Alabama. The Kentucky State Guard also camped on the exposition grounds for the drills.

The exposition added more pictures in the Art Gallery, making the collection distinctly American and one of the best in the west or south. The exposition added several pieces of statuary made by Kentucky sculptor Joel T. Hart, including his *Triumph of Chastity*.

As mentioned earlier, Cappa's Seventh Regiment Band returned for another season, but during the second half of the exposition, Patrick Gilmore's Band provided the musical entertainment. Gilmore, a composer and bandmaster, was born on December 25, 1829, in Ballygar, County Galway, Ireland. John Phillip Sousa regarded Gilmore as the "Father of the American Band." In 1849, he moved to the United States and settled in Boston, Massachusetts. In 1855, he gave the first Promenade Concert in America, which was the forerunner to today's Boston Pops orchestra. In 1858, he founded Gilmore's Band and enlisted with the 24th Massachusetts Volunteers. While serving in the Union army, he wrote the lyrics to "When Johnny Comes Marching Home," which he took from an old Irish antiwar folk song entitled "Johnny I Hardly Knew Ye." He also wrote "We Are Coming Father Abraham" and the famous "22nd Regiment March." After bands were disbanded, Massachusetts governor John Andrew enlisted Gilmore to reorganize military music making, and Union general Nathaniel Banks made him bandmaster general. After the war, Gilmore organized in 1869 the National Peace Jubilee, and in 1872, the World's Peace Jubilee and International Musical Festival, which brought him the reputation as one of the leading musical figures in America. At the World's Peace Jubilee, he organized a two-thousand-piece orchestra and a twenty-thousand-voice chorus. In 1873, Gilmore left Massachusetts for New York, becoming the bandmaster of the 22nd Regiment. He created Gilmore's Concert Garden, which became the first Madison Square Garden. In 1876, he was the musical director for the centennial celebrations in Philadelphia. In 1878, Gilmore traveled Europe with his band.[41] He also started the tradition of greeting the new year at Times Square in New York.

The five-hundred-member chorus also returned to the exposition, and on Thursday nights, the exposition decided to put on huge fireworks displays, provided by Paine & Company of London, England. The concluding device of the display was the "Arc de Triumphe" and "Bois de Boulogne," which was 150 feet in length. The famous device of the "Sacred White Elephant," which stood for the Republican Party, was produced in which the huge beast walked with a natural and lifelike

A stereograph of the Alabama Exhibit at the Southern Exposition, hosted by the Louisville & Nashville Railroad. *Courtesy of the New York Public Library.*

movement across the grounds. Among the many other devices were the "Falls of the Niagara," which was 30 feet long, and the "Dragon," which moved along the ground. After the final device, there was a flight of 250 of the largest rockets. There were also colossal fire portraits, measuring 50 by 30 feet, of the presidential candidates of that time and of local celebrities. A grand naval combat, with vessels measuring 130 feet long combated each other. There was Athens's Temple of Fame, which changed to the abode of Pluto; they were designed from originals in the British Museum. There was also the "Bombardment of Alexandria" and many other pyrotechnic devices, which were shown at night to on-looking visitors. The iron tower, with the ten electric lights, was turned off for the fireworks displays.[42]

Another change made to the exposition was the galleries, in which no exhibits were allowed; they were replaced with museums and eateries. On the southeast corner of the building stood a museum, on the northeast corner was George Brown's restaurant, on the southwest corner was Henry Israel's bar and in the southeast was George Brown's lunch stand. At the top of the hill, near the Art Gallery was the fruit stand owned by Charles Scholtz.

In the center of the building, Thomas Edison's workmen erected an electric fountain in the center of the building. The fountain stood thirty-five feet tall and around the top was a coronet of seventy-five Edison lamps, with white and red lights, backed up with white flower-shaped shades. Underneath the coronet, the shaft was covered with iridescent metal, in which the metal's glow was intensified by the lights. Below that, there was a perforated crown supporting rocks, ferns, mosses and vines. From the perforated crown was a cascade of water, which descended into larger and larger cascades before falling into a spray in a catch basin. Under the water, there were multicolored electric lights. The landscaping in the fountain was done by Louisville florists Nanz and Neuner; Mr. L. Stieringer of the Edison Company designed the fountain. In addition to the five thousand Edison electric lights, many of the exhibitors added their own lights, and the Edison Company also had their own exhibit.[43]

In order for everyone to attend the exposition, the board of directors decided to lower the admission on opening day from fifty cents to twenty-five cents; afterward, the price went back to fifty cents. A visitor could

A colorful lithograph of the Southern Exposition. The poster was given out to the public by a railroad company. *Courtesy of the Conrad-Caldwell House.*

purchase a season ticket for eight dollars for adults and five dollars for children twelve years or younger.

Some the exhibitors at the Southern Exposition are names that we still recognize today, such as the Baldwin Piano Company, American Express Company, Kentucky Institute for the Blind and the American Printing House for the Blind.

On August 16, the Southern Exhibition of 1884 was ready to open to the public. On opening day, the weather was sunny and perfect. At 2:00 p.m., Governor J. Proctor Knott of Kentucky arrived from Frankfort to the Louisville station. The governor would have arrived earlier but a train car jumped the track, and the debris had to be cleared before his train could pass. Knott brought with him Secretary of State McKenzie, Attorney General P.W. Hardin, Treasurer James W. Tate, Commissioner of Agriculture John F. Davis and Private Secretary Kincaid. The reception committee consisted of President Bennett Young; Judge J.W. Barr; Dr. Elisha David Standiford; ex-mayor John Baxter, who served from 1879 to 1881; Nathaniel Bloom; and H. Verhoff Jr. Dr. Elisha Standiford served as a member of the Kentucky Senate from 1868 to 1871 and served in Congress from 1873 to 1875. After leaving Congress, he became president of the Louisville and Nashville Railroad from 1875 to 1879. Louisville's largest airport was originally named after Dr. Standiford. The four open carriages proceeded to Alexander Hotel, where they dined. Shortly after 3:00 p.m., the party left for city hall; General Taylor of the mounted police escorted their carriages. Other carriages followed the procession, including carriages carrying ex-Kentucky governor Blackburn; General John Echols; Merriweather Lewis Clark Jr.; Bidermann DuPont; Colonel S. Lyford, chairman of the United States Commissioners; T.S. Hill, United States commissioner; Major Schaumberg, United States commissioner; Buckingham and Hazen, United States commissioners; Attorney General P.W. Hardin; Colonel Stoddard Johnston; Joshua Bullitt Jr.; and W. Churchill. Johnston, in addition to helping establish the Kentucky Press Association, served as Kentucky's secretary of state from 1875 to 1879. He was known as a political writer and orator and was one of the leading forces in Kentucky's Democratic Party.

At 4:00 p.m., the party arrived at the exposition at the Fourth Street entrance. They filed out of their carriages and out to the Music Hall, where they were received by General John B. Castleman. As they entered, Cappa's band played the Southern Exposition March, a composition dedicated to the Louisville Press Club. The crowd that had gathered at the Music Hall cheered for the governor, his party and the reception committee. Once they all took their seats, the band subsided, and Colonel Bennett Young arose to announce that the ceremonies had begun. The Reverend T.D. Witherspoon gave the opening prayer. Afterward, Professor Schueler's chorus sang a song. After the song, Colonel Young delivered his speech. During the speech, he complimented the people of Louisville for their successful accomplishment in presenting to the world "typical Southern progress and Southern energy" and their capacity, as a "Southern people," for organizing and maintaining the huge commercial undertaking involved in the Southern Exhibition.[44] He commemorated Louisville's achievements in development and progress. As he stated,

Louisville citizens "may point to events now occurring with extraordinary frequency, marked by the exhibition of forces which stamp her people with the seal of true improvements and which entitles her to a front rank among the progressive cities of this wonderful country."[45] As he expressed in his speech, Louisville's seal was the motto Progress. During his speech, Young recognized that thirty counties of Indiana and eighty counties of Kentucky had exhibits at the exposition. He mentioned that, in the Art Gallery, Kentucky sculptor and artist Joel T. Hart's *Woman Triumph* was the "most beautiful work of sculpture ever chiseled by an American hand." He pointed out that the federal government also recognized the magnitude and importance of the exposition by bringing numerous national treasures from every department. Young gave credit to the exposition for being the first to be lighted with electricity. He concluded his speech stating:

> *To such an Exposition, the best and greatest of its kind, with a distinguished past and a brilliant future, the management and the city of Louisville invite the people of this country…And now in behalf of the directory, I present this Exposition to the Mayor of Louisville. It is fitting that, as chief executive of this city, you should receive this work of our hands and give official sanction to its inauguration before it shall be formally declared opened by the Chief Executive of the State of Kentucky.*[46]

A large roar broke out among the audience, and when the applause subsided, President Young arose again and stated that Mayor Jacob was ill and could not attend, but that Colonel George Baber would read the mayor's address. After reading Jacob's speech, Governor J. Proctor Knott arose and gave his speech. Born on August 29, 1830, in Kentucky, Governor Knott moved to Missouri in 1850 to start his political career. From 1859 to 1861, he served as Missouri's attorney general. In 1861, he resigned from office when he refused to swear an oath of allegiance to the federal government. The state of Missouri disbarred Knott and imprisoned him for a brief time. In 1863, he returned to Kentucky and was elected to the U.S. House of Representatives. In 1871, he made a notable speech ridiculing a bill to subsidize westward expansion of railroads. His Duluth speech was reprinted in several publications and brought to Knott national attention. In 1875, he returned to the House of Representatives and served as chairman of the judiciary committee. In 1883, Knott left Congress and ran for governor, which he won. In 1892, he became a professor at Centre College, and in 1894, he helped organize the college's law school.[47]

In his speech at the exposition, he pointed out that the displays on view were not from the spoils of war but from peace. He also supported Mayor Jacob's speech by reinforcing the notion that Kentucky's natural resources rivaled that of any country. After the governor's speech, the exposition opened to the crowds, and by 8:30 p.m., over fifteen thousand visitors had entered the building. The visitors were delighted to see the new fountain, with the seventy-five different colors reflected in the water by the electric lights. As darkness approached, the crowd was amazed as the five thousand Edison lights came on gradually inside the building.

At 9:00 p.m., A.S. Willis and Kentucky secretary of state James A. McKenzie gave a speech to the crowd. In McKenzie's speech, he remarked how Kentucky was tied with the commercial realm, and that he was glad to see Louisville placed "in the commercial sisterhood of the Union." He concluded his speech, again praising Louisville.

In his final remarks, he said:

> *Go on brave city, in your effort to canonize labor! Make the world acquainted with the skill of your handicraftsmen: extend to all the open palm of Kentucky hospitality and welcome. Let your resources rather than your importunities invite the world to share your fortunes, and still further add to the prestige of your glory.*[48]

Cappa and his Seventh Regiment Band gave a concert in the morning and evening. During the afternoon concert, the Southern Exposition March was played, followed by the overture of "The Martyr's" and pieces from the operas of Meyerbeer. Alessandro Liberati played "Blue and Gray," after which the audience erupted in applause. Liberati was an eminent cornet virtuoso. He was born in Frascati, near Rome, Italy. At an early age, he studied the coronet and served in the Papal Guard in the Vatican; he later served in the French Foreign Legion as a musician. In 1872, he came to North America and served for three years as bandmaster of artillery and soloist to the Earl of Dufferin, Canada. From 1875 to 1877, he was bandmaster of the Detroit National Guard in Michigan.[49] After Liberati's performance, Verdi's "Tempest of the Heart" was played on a euphonium. The five-hundred-person chorus sang the bridal chorus from "Lohengrin," and the national hymn "America." During the evening concert, the chorus sang "The Heavens are Telling" by Handel. The highlight of the evening was "Lucia de Lammermoor." During the exposition, two concerts were held daily; one in the afternoon and one in the evening.

In the Art Gallery, Joel T. Hart's *Woman Triumphant*, *The Morning Glory* and *The Reproof* were on display. Hart was born in Kentucky in 1810. His parents were poor and received very little academic education. As a young man, he learned the profession of a stonemason and built walls and chimneys; later, he began to carve stone and marble, working as a stonecutter. He studied anatomy at Transylvania University in Lexington, Kentucky. Later in life, he formed a friendship with Henry Clay, and Hart made a bust of him. In 1849, Hart traveled to Florence, Italy, to complete his statue of Clay, which he made for the Ladies Clay Association of Richmond, Virginia. His next work was a bronze statue of Clay, which stands in New Orleans, and later, he sculpted a marble statue of Clay, which stands in the Jefferson County Courthouse. He also made busts of Andrew Jackson, John J. Crittenden and others. He died in March 1877 in Florence.[50]

American artist Seymour Joseph Guy (1824–1910) displayed his *Richelieu*; *See-Saw Margery Daw*, which represented a mother and child at bedtime; *Mother and Child*; and *Open Your Mouth and Shut Your Eyes*, which depicts a little girl holding a strawberry before a half-nude infant lying on the floor. The exposition had Francis D. Millet's (November 3, 1846–April 15, 1912) *Reading of the Story of Oenone*, which received praise from the New York critics and was sent to the New York Academy exhibition. A number of citizens from Detroit later bought the painting. The painting depicts four Greek maidens, three of whom are listening to the fourth, who is reading the story. As for foreign artists, Rosa Schweininger of Munich displayed her *The Old Antiquary*, and Edouard de Beaumont's (1821–1888) had the *Temptation of St. Anthony*. In the east gallery, the exposition displayed Marie Francoise Constance Mayer's *The Evangeline* and *Song of the Shirt*. American artist Benoni Irwin's (1840–1896) portrait of *Albert Fink* was, according to the *Louisville Courier-Journal*, one of the most successful portraits in the country. German American landscape artist Albert Bierstadt (January 30, 1830–February 18, 1902) had his *Wahsach Mountains* on display, and American artist Harry Chase (1853–1889) showcased his *View of Battery Park*. American artist Hugh Bolton Jones (1848–1927) displayed his *Hering River*, which at the time was one of the finest landscape portraits exhibited in the National Gallery. In the east gallery, American realist painter Gilbert Gaul's (1855–1919) *Silenced* represented a recently deserted battlefield on a moonlight night in winter. Dead bodies were strewn on the ground, and a dismembered cannon stands in the middle distance. The moon is not visible, but the moonlight falls upon the snow, glistens on a weapon and parts of the cannon. A wounded soldier, left for dead, has regained consciousness and partly raised himself on his left arm. A dead soldier lays in the foreground.[51]

F.L. Kirkpatrick displayed his *Benvenuto Cellini Unveiling the Statue of Perseus*. The exposition had, in the west gallery, Eastman Johnston's (July

A sketch of the interior of the Art Gallery at the Southern Exposition. *Courtesy of the* Louisville Courier-Journal.

A sketch of the Art Gallery and fountain in Central Park, *Harper's Weekly*. *Courtesy of the Ken Maguire Collection.*

29, 1824–April 5, 1906) *The Funding Bill*, which was considered at the time the finest picture in the country. (Johnston, an American artist, was the cofounder of the Metropolitan Museum of Art in New York City.) The painting depicted two businessmen engaged in conversation. The exposition also showcased American artist P.P. Ryder's (March 19, 1847–March 28, 1917) painting, *Warming Up*, which showed an old man sitting in front of the stove on a cold morning drinking a freshly made cup of coffee. American figure and portrait artist George F. Fuller (January 17, 1822–March 21, 1884) displayed his *Forest in Normandy*, which depicted a road passing through the woods, along with two peasants passing through. Arthur Preston also had his *Nightfall*, which showed a number of sheep on top of a hill at sunset.

Another one of the new exhibits was the Madison County, Kentucky historic and pioneer exhibit. Colonel R.T. Durrett of Louisville presented the county with a copy of the original pioneer map of the state, drawn by John Filson, under the supervision of Daniel Boone, William Kennedy and other noted hunters. As part of the exhibit, the commissioners showed the best pioneer maps of Lincoln, Jefferson and Fayette Counties. A plat of the John Swift Silver Mine, found among the papers of an "eminent pioneer," was part of the display. Of course, no one has ever found the John Swift Silver mine. As the local paper of the time pointed out, the location of the mine was claimed by every county in eastern Kentucky. Madison County also displayed rare books on Kentucky's history, including early state school and textbooks.

Once the exposition opened, very few visitors knew about the rate of admission being lowered from fifty cents to twenty-five cents, so the board of directors decided to have "cheap days" on every Monday and Saturday.

Lieutenant Buckingham of the U.S. Navy brought artifacts from the Greely exploration party. The State Department built a circular-shaped exhibit, which was supposed to represent the world. The display was divided into five sections, which represented the five great geographical divisions of the world, such as Africa, America, Asia, Australia and Europe. The purpose of the display was to illustrate the resources of the world and to show the channels for the development of the world's industrial and commercial industry. The display also showed the role the United States played in world commerce. In front of the display was a globe of the world. Over the space of each continental group were flags hung over the principal countries. The State Department hung the flags, in order to form a canopy over the entire display. A large map of each geographical division contained illuminated letters, which stated the countries' commercial statistics in each division. Under the Diplomatic Department, the civil, social and religious statistics of the countries were represented in the display. Under the Consular Department, the industrial and commercial features of each country were displayed. For an example, Japan had an embroidered and painted screen showing its tea industry and another screen showed their rice industry. Of course, the State Department made sure that the cotton industry of the world was on display, in keeping with the Southern Exposition theme. The cattle industry was also displayed. Egypt had the earthenware display. An electric chandelier with colored globes hung over the display to illustrate the glass-making industry.

The United States Postal Service had a display at the exposition. The exhibit contained samples of all items used by the post office. The old methods of carrying the mail were represented by models of mail coaches and carriers on horseback. The collection of stamps showed all the varieties issued since stamps replaced the old franking system. The display contained models of United States mail steamboats, and ocean vessels that carried mail from the United States to foreign countries. The various types of pouches used were exhibited and the instruments used in the interiors of post offices. The display was a functioning post office, and visitors could use the facilities for transactions of all kinds of postal business.

The Bureau of Education also had an exhibit. The exhibit was located in the northwest section of the building. In the cases, visitors found various publications of the bureau, giving educational statistics, circulars and papers, along with special and important topics connected with education, such as school laws, industrial education and stenography. A large revolving case devoted itself to the study of botany and contained mounted botanical specimens and a variety of woods, each being mounted in three different ways, in order to show the characteristics of the grain and color. The kindergarten case displayed objects used in the best classrooms, including a number of miniature household implements used in teaching and illustrating the principles of physics. There were also geological specimens and tools used in botany and a number of small instruments used in school gymnasiums. There were objects used in teaching weights and measurements of the metric system. Another case displayed samples of sewing, which were done by girls from age ten to thirteen in the Winthrop school of Boston, Massachusetts, and gave examples of their handiwork, such as boys' suits. In some of the frames were a number of mechanical drawings from the Worchester Free Institute of Massachusetts. The display showed how the students were taught to do decorative mechanical work. The panels contained photographs illustrating the Massachusetts School of Technology, giving views of the main workrooms in the school. Twelve panels contained charts for teaching the various trades and industrial pursuits; other panels contained charts for teaching physiology; and five pictures illustrated the Bellevue Hospital (New York) Training School for Nurses. Globes, maps, object lesson charts and pictures of eminent educators finished out the exhibit.

As the visitor entered the Fourth Street entrance, they immediately noticed the electric fountain in the center. On the right of the fountain was the first display case, which contained samples of raw cotton from around the world—divided into every grade and variety—that was collected by an English firm and provided by Louisville native H.P. Forwood.

The next case on the right of the fountain was a display of art needlework, made by Fannie Freeman, of Louisville. The display included everything from a pin cushion cover to a doll's dress to an embroidered screen. There was the display of Mr. McKnight, a carpet man, who displayed carpets, rugs and tapestries. The most expensive velvet carpets, the moquets, Brussels and artistic Eastern rugs hung together. At the display of Escott & Sons, dealers in art goods and interior decorations, they had beautiful mantels and grates. The mantels were made of ash, rosewood, mahogany, walnut and cherry. The floor of the exhibit was made of inlaid hardwood. J. Dulfinger had a porcelain and glassware display, which included Sevres, Dresden ware, Venetian and Florentine glass and Royal Worchester. At the corner of the Music Hall was the display of Nanz & Neuner florists, who supplied a variety of fresh flowers and plants for sale.

Starting back at Fourth Street entrance and walking to the left, the visitor saw the post office display and then the display of Kendrick & Sons, who exhibited jewelry, bronzes, vases, bronze and brass busts, table silverware, oxidized silver and artistic lamps. There were mirrors, colored glassware and gold objects. The next display was F. Garafolo, manufacturer of shell jewelry and seller of artistic trinkets. At the end of the aisle was Ehrmann & Co., who sold candy. In the center of the eastern aisle was an exhibit provided by the Lampson Cash Railway, which displayed Chinese and Japanese art. The display contained one thousand items picked up by the company, which bought and sold goods of Chinese and Japanese manufacture. Pottery, table porcelain and Chinese wares were on display; Japanese curios filled the cases. There was also Dresden china, European and American manufacture and wax matches.

On the other side of the eastern aisle, on the other side of the fountain, was the display of furniture dealers Bennett Brothers & Co., followed by the booth containing Japanese women selling products from their country and the display of Shulhafer, a plumber. The display space was filled with chandeliers. Some Moorish and antique patterns graced the display, along with brass and bronze. An artistic shaped lamp, with heavy pieces of blue glass sunk into the brass, hung in the display. Also in the area was the display of the Louisville Agricultural Company, makers of plows and other agricultural implements. On the other side of the aisle was the exhibit of plow manufacturer Thomas Meikles & Co., with the display rotating with a number of small plows, harvesters, rollers, etc., that drew over a circle of earth, demonstrating their function on a farm. The display even had a sheet of water, in which several steamboats went by, and the building of a toy house was in the center, which sat in a garden. Following that exhibit, there was the display of A.B. Barney, dealer in oriental goods, such as Turkish pipes, scented woods carved into various patterns and Eastern jewelry; the Clark Mile End Spool Cotton Company made a display of colored spool cotton, piled into a pyramidal shape, in which the shades of color were graded; the Louisville Lithograph Company decorated a room with lithographs and business cards; and Ponder & Co.'s exhibit consisted of jewelry, artistic designs in bronze and table silver and cutlery. At the corner of the two center aisles was the stand of a maker of artificial flowers. In the center of the western main aisle was Springer & Co., which sold soda water. Next came the display of T.C. Tracey, who exhibited silver, both hammered and oxidized, and gold filigree work; Selah Mousur's stand sold Jerusalem relics and Oriental goods; B.F. Avery sold Waterbury watches; and Thomas Payne had a large display of celluloid goods, from combs to a complete outfit for furnishing a house with goods. The last display was T. Conti, a glass blower.

The display made by Dr. John Bull was one of the more unique exhibits at the exposition. The display consisted of a large case of ebony-finished wood, decorated with silver trimmings and fitted like an elaborate parlor; in the center was a life-sized bull made of bottles containing Dr. Bull's famous remedies. The bottles were fastened with a wire frame. Over the bull hung a chandelier of electric lights decorated with artificial flowers and vines. Chairs and sofas near the display, which was found on the north end of the east side, gave a comfortable area for visitors to rest.[52]

Around the corner of the aisle was the Crab Orchard Salts Company. The display contained enough of the Lincoln County product to keep all Louisville residents in good digestive health. The bottles of liquid salts and boxes of the crystal salts piled into pyramids, around which placards were placed, proclaiming the virtues of the salts remedies.[53]

In the same aisle, but closer to the Fourth Street entrance, was the display of Sharpe & Middleton of New York, which comprised several large glass cases devoted to carpets and tapestries. The rugs were made of animal skins, such as foxes, bears and leopards. Axminister carpets, heavy embroidered velvet and silk-made plush table covers, along with moquette carpets, madras portiers, Wilton carpets, ingrain carpets and Brussels carpets were also on display in the large glass case. Another case contained a variety of gowns, underwear, cloaks, linen; another contained silk, satin and woolen dress goods; while yet another case had Parisian novelties in toilet articles.[54]

J.C. Goldbach's display consisted of fine leather for boots, shoes and gaiters; it also contained finished boots and shoes, shoemaker's tools, and tanner's and currier's tools and contained hides.

Mantle & Cowan displayed oak-tanned leather, leather belting and dealers in foreign and domestic leather and mill supplies. Around the partition, which enclosed the exhibit space, there were large hides, including sole leather, while hides were lighter and finished in black on one side. The exhibit of leather contained every type of example, from a bull's hide to the French kid. They also displayed tanner's tools and materials. The display contained complete outfits for saddler's shops and boot makers, including all kinds of sewing machines to make finished boots and shoes. The company also had an exhibit for H.W. John asbestos materials, including liquid paints, oils, roofing materials, packing for steam pipes and fireproof materials. The Tanite Company displayed steam engines, steam pumps, engine oils, rubber and leather belting, hose, copper and iron wire and a variety of ropes. Myers & Bonn were makers of harnesses and saddles and dealers in saddle materials; the company's display cases included single and double harnesses, fine saddles, whips, carriage rugs, horse blankets and stable outfits.[55]

The National Museum set up an exhibit at the exposition, located on the western half of the north aisle of the building. The most noticeable feature of the exhibit was a large whaleboat, fully rigged with set sails, oars, harpoons and lances. On the bow of the ship was an old swivel gun, which was used to shoot a harpoon into the whale. A painting represented a whaleboat's crew taking a whale at the wharf and boiling out the oil from the blubber. In a glass case, there was a model of a fully rigged whaling ship, with a sperm whale lying alongside, from which men were cutting and hoisting the blubber to the deck; a fully rigged fishing schooner; and a Chinese warship, with set sails, oars, boats, guns and pikes on board.[56]

The exhibit also described the fishing industry in America, with a number of photographs showing the processes of catching, preparing, canning and shipping American sardines, or herring. The lobster industry and cod industry were also illustrated with photographs. There were illustrations of the fisheries in New England. The National Museum made plaster casts of white fish and showed how they were packed and frozen in Michigan.

The Natural Museum showcased the factories for making glue and fertilizer, which were made out of menhaden fish. There were examples of fish glue made from the skin and bladders of cod and hake. Other cases showed fans and other fancy ornaments made from various bird feathers; what could be done with shells, such as jewelry, buttons, and umbrella handles; and an illustration of the glove making industry. The textile industry of America and other countries were also illustrated. In a separate display, there was a collection of silks presented in 1855 to Commodore Matthew C. Perry by the Japanese government. Another collection had silk that was presented to the Smithsonian by the Portuguese Centennial Commission. The manufacture of cotton goods in the United States, such as hemp, jute, grass goods, flax and other fabrics, were showcased.

The museum also displayed photographs of Egyptian and Assyrian artifacts, the originals being housed in the British Museum. The collection included water birds of America, two cases containing plaster casts of snakes and other reptiles of North America, along with turtles and tortoises in another.[57]

Southwest of the fountain was the exhibit of M&J Ginoris, manufacturer and importer of artificial flowers and plants. The introduction of artificial plants only occurred recently in America before the exposition opened. The artificial plants were made with cotton cloth covered with a solution of rubber after being painted to represent the natural plant. To reproduce the velvet appearance of a begonia, velvet was actually used.

Just south of the fountain was an exhibit of Charles Friedl, proprietor of Kentucky's first decorative pottery. The display included hand-decorated tables, chamber and toilet sets, plaques and vases. Every form of handmade decorations was applied to china ware of every style. The Carpenter Annear & Company, located south of the electric fountain, displayed a line of galvanized iron cornice work, tin, slate and tile roofing and corrugated iron roofing and siding. Two nine-foot-high statues made of copper, representing winter and summer and manufactured for the courthouse in Lafayette, Indiana, were on display; another nine-foot-high statue, representing justice, stood in front of the exhibit. The Detroit White Bronze Company, located near the post office and the Fourth Street entrance, displayed cemetery work, including statuary, portraits, busts and medallions of prominent people; the material used was pure zinc.

Powell & Douglas of Waukegan, Illinois, exhibited hunting and pleasure boats, which were adapted to be used in any type of water. The firm built the largest variety of boats made in the country, from a shell weighing twenty-eight pounds to a steam pleasure yacht fifty feet long. They also exhibited their champion windmill, which was used in the most of the west.[58]

The I.F. Stone & Sons Company of Louisville exhibited their Edward Storm Company side bar, springs and gears for carriages of every description. The gear, with body fastenings, was exhibited in every shape, both plain and intricate. J.C. Oliver of Louisville showed their patented, improved buggy top in its skeleton stage alongside the finished product. The N.D. Hunter & Company of Louisville exhibited carriage material of every description, including a variety of large buggies, wagons and cart wheels, hubs and spokes made by the Keyas Manufacturing Company of Terra Haute, Indiana.[59]

Simon Shulhafer exhibit, located on the main aisle, near the Sixth Street entrance, displayed the newest designs in chandeliers, lamps and all gaslight goods. None of the designs had been exhibited in the west before. Every imaginable tint, color and form of glass was on the display. There were also useful articles among them, such as the latest sanitary wash and water closets.[60]

One of the added attractions to the exposition was a roller coaster, installed by W.B. Warren. Thousands of visitors took advantage of it. Visitors, both adults and children, enjoyed the "sleigh ride down hill without the snow."

The exposition formed a decoration committee to make sure that the residents along Fourth, Second and Sixth Streets and the streets crossing them decorated their houses with flags and bunting. The committee members also made sure that the streets at night had Chinese lanterns and gaslights. The *Louisville Courier Journal* stated: "no good citizen will fail to respond to their (the committee's) request."[61]

Along the hill, skirting the southern portion of the exposition fairgrounds, the state guard companies set up their tents at Camp Proctor Knott. At 5:00 a.m. on August 20, 1884, the men arose from their white tents, and after a squad drill an hour later, the grounds were filled with squads of men going through their manual of arms. At 7:45 a.m., the surgeon's call was sounded, and Lieutenant Colonel D.W. Yandell, medical director of the brigade, started his rounds. No one was sick from the hot march from the evening before, and the surgeon and his staff left the grounds. At 10:00 a.m., the company began to drill. After drill, the men were allowed to eat dinner and roam the grounds or the exposition. At 3:45 p.m., the regimental bugles sounded for battalion drill. Companies formed and marched into line. Major Speed of the First Regiment, Major L.W. McKee of the Second Regiment and Colonel Crump of the Third Regiment marched to the drill grounds and showed off their tactics.

A large audience began to assemble around the grandstand to watch the regiments drill. After the battalion drill, the regiments were marched up in front of the grandstand for the dress parade. Visitors rode up in their carriages, and a great many spectators took to the grandstand to see the dress parade. Colonel John B. Castleman, Lieutenant Colonel Yandell, the regimental commanders and staff officers were mounted on fine horses, in their finest uniforms. According to the *Courier-Journal*, the dress parade "was conducted with precision and accuracy of regular troops." After the troops marched back to camp, they received a communication from Bennett Young to Colonel John Castleman, inviting him and the state troops to a formal reception that night. Colonel Castleman wrote back that he would bring the troops at 8:00 p.m. The troops would return to camp at 10:30 p.m. for "Taps." Governor Knott also planned to be at the reception that night. At 5:00 p.m., he would review the Kentucky State Guard, and the usual drills and dress parade would take place. Colonel Castleman made arrangements for a sham battle.[62]

On August 20, at 8:00 p.m., the Seventh Regiment Band proceeded to the Fourth Street entrance to meet the state guard. A few minutes later, the crowd heard the beat of drums, and the troops began to arrive. As the men came on streetcars, the crowd had to wait until the entire state guard companies had arrived before they moved out for the reception. Governor Knott finished his meal at Camp Knott headquarters and arrived at the fairgrounds. A few minutes after 9:00 p.m., the men formed their lines, and the Seventh Regiment Band played the march from "Heart and Hand," as the troops moved into the building. Governor Proctor Knott marched in front of the troops, along with Lieutenant Colonel D.W. Yandell, Henry Watterson and Jesse Middleton. Colonel Castleman commanded the brigade. The men formed around the fountain. When the band stopped playing, Bennett Young stepped forward and welcomed the Kentucky State Guard. He told the assembled men that he was "pleased and honored" that they accepted his invitation. He told the men that the military history of Kentucky exemplified skill and heroism, and that on every battlefield in which they were engaged in combat, they were second to none "in all the highest and noblest attributes of soldiers."[63] He hoped that the young men of the guard would select Kentucky as their place of work and triumphs. He hoped that the guard would join the civilian visitors the following night and watch the firework displays. At the end of Young's speech, the Seventh Regiment Band played "Dixie," and the men cheered. When the band stopped playing, Colonel Castleman took off his cap and spoke to Bennett Young, thanking him and the exposition for allowing the Kentucky State Guard to come and enjoy the displays. After Colonel Castleman's reply, the commanders gave an order to break rank, and the soldiers dispersed in every direction and walked the grounds. At 10:00 p.m., the men fell into line and marched out, but some of the men promised to come back and see some of the ladies.[64]

At 4:00 p.m. on August 22, 1884, the members of the Louisville Legion held a sham battle. Thousands attended the event, and the Second and Fourth Streets' streetcars ran every three minutes to bring people to the grounds. The Legion charged fifty cents to witness the event, and the proceeds went toward the uniform fund. There were no battle plans, but the winner was determined by strategic movements. Colonel Castleman commanded one of the armies. During the mock Civil War battle, more than one thousand soldiers charged and retreated, countermarched and fixed bayonets. The smoke of battle, the roar of artillery and the rattle of musketry brought realism to the event. Officers barked orders, privates shuffled into line, with dust rising in clouds. Hoarse sergeants screamed at privates who got out of line. Suddenly a shot rang out and a soldier dropped to the ground. The soldier did not fall from a wound but of entirely too much whiskey. As the *Louisville Times* put it: "One heroic soldier was engaged in a contest with a bottle of whiskey and he was ingloriously defeated."[65]

On August 26, the first of the drill competitions began at the Exposition Fairgrounds. The drills occurred at 3:00 p.m. and lasted until 6:00 p.m., when the soldiers readied for dress parade. Cappa's Seventh Regiment Band accompanied each company in their march from the camp to the drill grounds and also furnished the music for the parades. Because of the special military drills, the exposition did not hold concerts for the three days during the competition. There were six companies that participated in the drills, and two companies drilled each day; the order in which the companies were chosen was by lot by the committee. The judges who conducted the drills and parades were Major Joseph Breckinridge, U.S. Army; Captain W.S. Edgerley of the U.S. Seventh Cavalry; First Lieutenant Edgar S. Dudley of the U.S. Artillery; and Second Lieutenant John W. Thompson of the same regiment.[66]

For two weeks, the exposition employed a large number of men with plows, carts, scrapers, harrows and a herd of mules to level and grade the ground enclosed by the quarter-mile track, running on the amphitheater on the south side of the building. The drill grounds were made to have a slight grade in order for the water to drain into a large pipe that ran beneath the track and stand. The Southern Exposition not only had the best drill grounds in the United States but also had the best bicycle track, stock display grounds and fireworks grounds in the United States.[67]

Advertisement for the bicycle tournament at the Southern Exposition. *Courtesy of the* Louisville Courier-Journal.

The state guard moved their tents from Camp Knott to Central Park and was to be occupied by the military companies that entered the drill completion. The Brookfield Rifles formed in 1882. The Porter Rifles of Nashville formed in 1875, and when they marched to the field, they were accompanied by the Burns Tennessee Light Artillery, the Harding Light

Artillery and the Hermitage Guards. The Montgomery Grays, of the Second Regiment of the Alabama State Guard, formed in 1860. During the outbreak of the war, the company joined the Sixth Alabama Infantry and served throughout the entire Civil War. In 1860, they had 120 men, but by the end of the war, there were only 1 corporal and 6 men left. After the war, the company reorganized. The Indianapolis Light Infantry formed in 1877.[68]

On the day of the drill, the street parade of the military companies opened the event, and people crowded Main Street and the other streets to see the state guards. General Taylor of the Louisville Police, along with a company of policemen, escorted the troops. Eichhorn's band played several selections in the rotunda at the Louisville Hotel before the troops formed their lines, and later, the band played martial music during the parade. The Porter Rifles and Montgomery Grays did not participate in the parade since they drilled earlier in the day. Between five and six thousand people witnessed the military drills. The prizes to be awarded would be done at dress parade.[69]

The Porter Rifles were the first to drill, followed by the Montgomery Grays. The criteria for the drill was the inspection of the company and their arms and accoutrements. The formation of the company and inspection covered nine movements and was conducted by the judges. The Manual of Arms, with the numbers given by the commander, covered twenty movements. The men conducted facing steps, alignments and firings. At the twenty-sixth number, the company began the movements by single rank, in which the wheelings, oblique marches, left and right turns and flank movements had to be carried out with perfect precision. The men moved in double rank and in columns of four with the various and complicated changes, including the rear in quick and double time, the oblique movements and wheelings in four in circle and back again. The platoon movement featured a drill where every formation of the company was presented in double time without change or halt.[70]

The men also performed a formation of a line, during which a continuous march and breaks to the front in columns of platoon and company were carried out. After the movement, the men closed with a march in line, single rank, during which three numbers of the manual were carried out without halting or a change of front. The 140 men were given forty-five minutes to carry out the schedule of movements.[71]

By 7:00 p.m., after the Porter Rifles left the field, the Quapaws took to the drill ground. Darkness surrounded the grounds, except the drill area, which was illuminated by the light bulbs from the electric tower. The *Louisville Courier-Journal* reported that perhaps for the first time in the annals of military history, a dress parade was held by electric light.[72] When the Quapaws formed on the field, Cappa's band played down the line.

After the drills were completed, the companies formed for dress parade, and the order to break rank was given. The fireworks display soon began, with the "Siege of Paris" and the "Storming of the Bastille" being the highlights of the fireworks program; the concluding fireworks display would be "The Angel of Peace." The amphitheater, which surrounded the parade grounds, seated fifteen thousand people and provided the visitors a full view of the fireworks display. At its end, Cappa's band played a battle piece. The Louisville Legion, with artillery and infantry, assisted Cappa's Seventh Regiment Band in the presentation. Bombs and rockets were fired during the concert. Cappa's work was entitled "America's Battle Piece" and dedicated to the state guard. Cappa also played "The American Bugler," composed by Alessandro Liberati and dedicated to Colonel John B. Castleman.[73]

The most successful day of the exposition occurred on August 29, 1884, when thirteen thousand people paid fifty cents to enter the building. In addition, over one thousand people entered on passes. An additional five to six thousand people came at night to see the activities. By the end of the day, over twenty thousand people had attended. When the drill contest began at 3:30 p.m., the exposition broke a record with the largest outdoor audience ever assembled in the west. The amphitheater was filled to capacity, and hundreds more stood around the guard ropes. The first state guard company to approach the field was the Treadway Reserves, wearing their gray uniforms and large white shakoes. After coming to parade rest in front of the judges' stand, Colonel Myers, commander of the Missouri State Guard, to which the Treadway Reserves belong, escorted Governor Thomas Crittenden of Missouri to a position in front of the company and presented the troops to him. The governor spoke to the men, telling them that the people of their state sent them to win the contest. He told every man to do their duty and then walked off the field. The men started with the Manual of Arms.[74]

Located at the judge's headquarters were a large number of Civil War veterans from both sides, and as the Treadway Guards warmed up, the old veterans gave expressions of surprise and admiration. When the company performed the battle manual of firing by file and rank, which followed with the movement of the men kneeling, the hand clapping turned into shouts, and the amphitheater broke out into loud and long applause. Next to enter the field was the Indianapolis Light Infantry, and they performed the Manual of Arms. The 140 movements took the Porter Rifles thirty-seven minutes to carry out; the Montgomery Grays, thirty-three minutes; the Quapaws, forty-one and one-half minutes; the Treadway Rifles, thirty-five minutes; and the Indianapolis Light Infantry, thirty-seven minutes.

At the close of the drill contest, all six companies marched onto the drill ground for inspection, review and dress parade. Major Breckinridge acted as inspector general, and after the companies were put into regimental formation, the line was inspected. When the command "by right in column of companies right wheel!" was given, each company swung around in perfect precision. The audience cheered. The regiment moved around the field in quick time, preceded by Cappa's Seventh Regiment Band, and when the order was given for "Double Quick," the columns of men went around again in "magnificent style."[75] At the end of the march, the dress parade took place, with Major Breckinridge as the chief officer.

The next day, on August 30, the crowd began to assemble in the amphitheater for the announcement of the winner of the military drill contest. At 6:00 p.m., the Treadway Reserves arrived on the field and gave an exhibition drill. They fired a couple of blank rounds from their rifles and performed some maneuvers. By 8:00 p.m., ten thousand people gathered in the amphitheater. At 8:05 p.m., Major Leathers, Colonel Faulkner, General Basil W. Duke and members of the military committee began to announce the prizes. They walked around the amphitheater, and General Duke called out the scores. First prize was the Treadway Reserves; second, the Montgomery Grays; third place was the Indianapolis Light Infantry; fourth was the Porter Rifles; and fifth was the Quapaw Guards. As the results were announced, the crowd "applauded vociferously."[76]

The results were posted in the *Louisville Courier-Journal* and stated that the Treadway Reserves scored 979 out of 1,000; the Montgomery Grays, 959; the Indianapolis Light Infantry, 953; the Porter Rifles, 926; and the Quapaw Guards, 909.[77]

After the announcement of the prizes, the Treadway Rifles came onto the field and fired a salute amid the applause of the people. After the conclusion of the prizes, the fireworks display began. The men and batteries were already located on the field, and band members were already seated under the light tower. The lights in the tower were turned off, and a large balloon with magnesium flares was set loose to light up the field for several minutes. Roman candles and other fireworks, including bombs and rockets, shot into the air. The fiery dragons that chased each other across the field and the whirling and shooting rings of fire all caused the crowd to cheer. A device lit up that said: "Welcome to the Kentucky Press." A huge elephant walked with a stately stride from one end of the field to the other, whisking his tail and moving its trunk with a lifelike appearance, bringing laughter and wonderment from the crowd. The elephant's color changed from one to another. The "Siege of Paris" and the "Storming of the Bastille" lit up, and the guns began to fire. The skirmishers on the northwest began to fire their muskets, and firing began on another part of the field in response. The roar of cannons could be heard, and the band played the "Marseilles." The firing of cannons and muskets grew louder as the troops marched in the direction of the fort. As the troops approached, the shots began to tell on the walls of the Bastille, and in places, they began to crumble and explode into flames. Martial music could be heard, and cannonading became louder. The bombs exploded against the walls of the prison, which burst into flames that shot high into the air. The walls crumbled, and as they fell away, the Goddess of Peace and Liberty appeared on the scene. A final flight of one hundred rockets, fired at once, closed the fireworks display. After the smoke cleared, Cappa's band played the battle piece, with fifty men and two field cannons used to accompany the music.[78]

Chapter 5

The Southern Exposition Becomes a World's Fair

On August 15, 1885, the Southern Exposition opened to a new season. The prominent business houses, from Main to Walnut, were dressed in flags and bunting. Fourth Street was already decorated, as well as many private residences. Business was suspended. Over ten thousand people filled the streets to watch the opening parade.

At 9:30 a.m., bells rung all over the city, and the factories blew their whistles. Thousands of little flags hung from every available window and cornice on main buildings. There were also long silk banners and streamers. Three companies of the Louisville Legion, the whole police force, fire departments and invited guests paraded through the streets. Adjutant General John B. Castleman formed the Louisville Legion at the Seventh Street Armory. At 1:30 p.m., General Castleman formed the men and marched the troops to Seventh and Jefferson Streets, where they were joined by the firemen and policemen. Chief Whallen commanded the police, and Major Hughes led the firemen. At 1:35 p.m., Governor J. Proctor Knott, Mayor Paul Booker Reed, Colonel Bennett Young, Colonel R.M. Kelly, Dr. Broadus, Colonel C.E. Sears, Major Clint McClarty, Major Tillman, Dr. Wathen, W.W. Hite Jr., Theodore Harris, J.L. Deppen, Samuel Russell and John Young Brown took the reviewing stand at the courthouse to review the parade. The police came first, preceded by Schneider's band. There were 150 men in the ranks.

The men formed in front of the platform, saluted, fell into platoons of eight and took up the line of march for the exposition, proceeding up Jefferson Street to Third and out Third to Magnolia Avenue. The fire department came next, and they were accompanied by George Kean, the young son of the former proprietor of the Louisville Hotel. Hook and Ladder Company No. 1 headed the procession, and Ladder Company 2 and Fire Telegraph Corps brought up the rear. The engines had been polished, and the horses were well groomed. The Charles Jacob and the Carey Blackburn, which were the names given to the fire engines, were also lavishly decorated. The Louisville Legion came last, preceded by the Legion band. The men wore brilliant uniforms and plumes. After saluting the governor, they marched out after the firemen and police.

At 3:00 p.m., the parade reached the exposition, and all the men disbanded.[79] The Louisville Legion entered the northern entrance of the grounds and, after saluting the gubernatorial party, they broke ranks on the eastern side; the fire department fell out at Magnolia Street. Several thousand people appeared at the courthouse and lined the streets from Fourth to Seventh. Several hundred people also stared out their windows as the parade went by their houses.[80]

The Reception Committee came out of the exposition building and formed two lines in front of the Fourth Street door. Dr. Griffiths headed the committee, along with J.T. Gathright, Milton H. Smith, J.W. Bayler, Colonel John Faulkner, Judge Edwards, ex-judge T.L. Burnett, Congressman Albert S. White, Captain John Weller, A.C. Lewis, John Callahan and Owen Galthright Jr. When the parade reached the carriage entrance to the exposition, the Legion band fell out of line and marched to the music stand. At the Fourth Street main entrance, a squad of exposition police met the parade. Schneider's military band followed and formed on each side of the walk. Next entered city police chief Whallen, who marched into the building. The Louisville Legion, commanded by General Castleman, marched in and formed a single line on the north walk. Dr. Griffith met Governor Knott at the gate and, along with the rest of the Reception Committee, walked into the music hall. John Young Brown and Mayor Reed also joined the governor and the Reception Committee on the stand. Applause broke out among the crowd when they saw the governor. After music stopped, the Reverend Dr. Broadus gave a prayer. After the prayer, Governor Knott gave a speech to the crowd. During his speech, he told the audience that the victories of peace outweighed the proudest achievements of military prowess. As for the exposition, he stated that the effects from the varied

> *trophies of peaceful industry upon the prosperity of our county, our State, or of this splendid city, which sits a star-like gem in the coronet of the Commonwealth, I need not speak. They have been so frequently demonstrated by the intelligence and liberality of Louisville that they have become patent to all. To refer to them would be but repeating a thrice fold tale. It simply remains for me, therefore, while wishing you, gentlemen exhibitors, the greatest possible prosperity, and for the great enterprise in which you are engaged, the largest measure of success, to declare, in compliance with the request of the management, the great Southern Exposition again formally opened.*[81]

After the applause, the Honorable Albert S. White came to the stage and introduced former U.S. Rep. John Young Brown of Kentucky. Brown was born on June 28, 1835, in Claysville, near Elizabethtown, Kentucky. Since his father, Thomas Dudley Brown, was a representative in the Kentucky legislature, he spent a good part of his youth at the Kentucky Capitol. In 1855, he graduated from Centre College and returned to Hardin County to study law. While practicing the bar, he gained a reputation as an exceptional orator. In 1859, despite not being the legal age to serve, he won a seat in the Kentucky House of Representatives. During the Civil War, he served as a colonel in the Confederate cavalry. In 1866, he was reelected to the state House of Representatives. Following his service, he returned to practice law in Louisville.[82]

During Brown's speech, he told the gathered audience that he was proud to be a Kentuckian. As for the exposition, he stated that:

> *if the youth of the State could, during the exposition, be taken, day after day, around its exhibits, and have explained to them whence these came, how made and for what used, it would prove of far greater practical value to them then anything could be taught, in the same length of time, from the text books of the schools. It would expand their minds, and give*

> *them a conception of the extent and imposing resources of their country, and the progress of the age in which they live.*[83]

He mentioned the variety of machines and the types of commercial goods on display, such as fruit, grains, lumber, coal, iron, gold and silver. He stated that every manufactured article found in the world markets was on display at the exposition. He stated that the public could witness a rare collection of paintings, located in the art gallery, which was located in Central Park, next to the exposition. Lakes, fountains and the shade of trees added to the beauty of the exposition. He told people that the exposition

> *is a poem-a revelation and an inspiration mingling in the chapter it opens the useful and the beautiful. The social commingling here will cause us to think better of ourselves and others, and the visit will promote the growth of knowledge-of taste-and of patriotism. It will be worthy to be raised as an event in life and its tones will leave pleasing echoes in the heart. If one come but for a day, it will be a pleasure won"* [84]

When Mr. Brown finished his speech, the orchestra under Walter J. Damrosch played the first concert of the season.[85]

Walter Damrosch was born in Bresian, Germany, on January 30, 1862. He was the youngest son of Leopold Damrosch, who was a distinguished composer and conductor who served as the lead violinist in the court orchestra at Weimar, an appointment given to him by Franz Lizst. At a young age, he studied piano and composition in Germany, but in 1871, Leopold Damrosch moved his family to New York. Walter continued to study under his father, serving as assistant conductor for his father's all-German season at the Metropolitan Opera in 1884 and 1885. On February 11, 1885, Damosch made his Metropolitan debut, conducting Wagner's "Tannhauser."[86]

The interior of the Southern Exposition was draped in flags and bunting. Bunting decorations hung from the roof of the rotunda in the center of the building to the main aisle. South of the center aisle was a mass of banners and flags of all nations; west of the building, there was a drapery over the woodwork and against the western wall of the building.

The Music Hall also was draped. Two large hanging United States flags crossed over the sounding shell. The railing of the gallery was in red, white and blue. The arms of the United States were hung against the cloth, and the windows were glazed with large transparent photographs belonging to the United States Geological Society and the Bureau of Ethnology.

When a visitor entered the Fourth Street entrance, behind the post office, the visitor encountered an Aztec temple in the Mexican exhibit. Around and in back of the temple were displays that came from France, Italy, Spain, the Orient, Russia and other foreign areas. The displays consisted of jewelry, rare curios, bric-a-brac, porcelain and other ornamental and artistic objects. Japanese exhibits were also prominent in the display. Louisville firms made displays of furniture, pianos, wallpaper and house decorations. In the western half of the aisle were more Oriental displays, gas fixtures, more pianos and a number of small exhibits. On the left, the

The Swiss chalet at the Southern Exposition. *Courtesy of the Conrad-Caldwell House.*

THE FISCHER PIANO,

—AND—

WHAT IS THOUGHT OF IT

BY EMINENT ARTISTS

Clara Louisa Kellogg :—"The 'Fischer Grand' pleased me exceedingly, and I find its tone pure and sympathetic, and of great sustaining quality."

Karl Merz :—"I cheerfully recommend the 'Fischer' Piano for all that is claimed for it."

Carl Zerrahn:—"It gives me the greatest pleasure to state that the 'Fischer' is a most excellent Piano."

Ivan E. Morowski:—"Your 'Grand' Piano is a noble instrument. Its voluminous tone, so brilliant, yet smooth and even."

Eugene Thayer :—"Except for large parlors, I prefer the Uprights to all other styles, and am glad to know of your immense trade. If it will assist you in the least, you are at liberty to quote my name morning, noon and night."

Will. S. Hays.—"I regard the 'Fischer' Piano as one of the best and sweetest toned instruments in the world. I am more than pleased with my Upright, and the more I use it, the better it seems to grow and the more delighted I am with it."

Back of an advertising card for the Fischer Piano Company, 1885. *Courtesy of the Ken Maguire Collection.*

Front of the advertising card for the Fischer Piano Company, 1885. *Courtesy of the Ken Maguire Collection.*

visitor encountered two spool thread exhibits. Visitors to the exhibition encountered a Turkish man selling items from Jerusalem, telling you that all his wares were at half price; the visitor could also encounter salesmen from China, Japan, Mexico, France, Germany or Italy. The exposition also built a full-scale Swiss chalet. The Pe-Kong exhibit was crowded with people who wanted to taste the Chinese tea.

The exposition still had the Kentucky display, but there were displays that included California and beyond, including Oriental ones with curious items from Persia, Jerusalem, Arabia, India and other Eastern countries. In the west area of the building was the United States Geological Society

The case that holds the Southern Exposition medal won by Thomas Brennan in 1885 for his sawmill. *Courtesy of the Brennan House, Louisville, Kentucky.*

A bronze plaque engraved with "Awarded by Southern Exposition Louisville Kentucky 1885 to Thomas Brennan for Best Sawmill and Sawmill Machinery." *Courtesy of the Brennan House, Louisville, Kentucky.*

Above: A rare photograph of the Brennan sawmill at the Southern Exposition. *Courtesy of the Brennan House, Louisville, Kentucky.*

Right: Southern Exposition medal won by Thomas Brennan for his sawmill display at the Southern Exposition. *Courtesy of the Brennan House, Louisville, Kentucky.*

Left: Painting of Thomas Brennan, who won a medal at the Southern Exposition in 1885 for his sawmill. *Courtesy of the Brennan House, Louisville, Kentucky.*

Below: The Brennan House, which is also the home of Preservation Louisville in Louisville, Kentucky. *Courtesy of the author.*

and Ethnology, which displayed paper, upholstering, dress cutting, jewelry, proprietary articles and wood. In the northern half of the west aisle, there was iron in various shapes, steel, buggies, carriages, wagons, carriage hardware, steel rails, hemp and twine, harness, agricultural and mechanical implements, coal, iron ore, oil cloths, plows, farm wagons, stoves and ranges. The agricultural implements extended farther down the aisle toward the south, where milling and other machinery were located.

In the southern half of the central aisle, there were displays from Austria and Hungary. Some of the additions made to the exposition were arc lights in the main building. An illustrated catalogue of the Art Gallery was for sale. Also, Company A of the Louisville Legion made its first appearance since its reorganization.

For the first time in the exposition's history, the viewing public experienced a full orchestra, provided by Walter J. Damrosch, where before the music was provided by a military band. The *Louisville Courier-Journal* stated that Damrosch "seemed to create the music, it came from him as it might have done from an enraptured composer. To watch him was to see the embodiment of the Spirit of Music."[87]

The exposition board made some changes to the Art Gallery. The changes included a wide range of subjects, and each exhibit was treated to different points of view, both in regard to the exhibitor's interpretation and technique. For example, there were over a dozen pictures of the sea. There was *Le Crepuscule* by Thomas Alexander Harrison and *The New Moon* by W. T. Richards. The two pictures portray the twilight setting over the open sea, but they are different.

The Mexican exhibit in the Aztec temple had thousands of items; Captain Luis Shiceo of the Mexican commission helped set up the display. The exhibit displayed the country's natural products, which could be used in the modern commerce of the day. In cases, there were hundreds of bottles of seeds and beans, along with a variety of plants. There were six hundred varieties of seeds, from coffee beans to vanilla beans to black-eyed peas. There were between seven and eight hundred different varieties of wood. Some of wood were shown for their usefulness while others were for their fragrance, such as sandalwood. There were fibrous plants such as hemp; jute; ixtle, which was a long, white fiber used for halters for horses and saddle bags; banana fibers; sacate escobiton, which was a kind of grass; and escobitillo, a large coarse grass. The palms and palmettos used for mats, baskets and other items were shown in their natural state, along with how they looked after they had been worked into useful items.

The Mexican exhibit had cotton plants, as well as a number of plants producing a fiber with the consistency of cotton. One of the interesting plants was the vegetable silk, which was soft, easily spun and warm as fur. Another silky fiber was the escobotillo, which grew on trees. The seed from the plant produced a chewing gum. Another fiber was the vegetable wool, as well as wool from Angora and merino goats. The silk from the mesquite worm was on display; the worm spins the silk in masses four or five feet long.

Also on display were Mexican handmade products, such as plain and decorated pottery, terra cotta figures, wax figures, clay figures dressed in native costume, birds of wax covered by the natural feathers of the animals, wax fruit, baskets and mats. The pottery came from the states of Jalisco, Michoacán, Pueblo and the Estado de Mexico. The local citizens of Mexico made the baskets, trays and tables by laying together bits of straw that were colored, and pictures were later added to the straw. The straw used in the tables was also used in brooms. The Mexican exhibit displayed a hemispherical vessel made from half of a gourd, which was polished, colored and varnished with an insect called the axe. The Pueblo made bits of carved onyx into fruit forms. There were also Mexican drinks, one of which was made from the chia seed. Another drink was made by soaking the Jamaica flower in water. Samples of paste made from prickly pear could be eaten by the public. The exhibit also had photographs of the country, which explained the character and helped the visitor take in a panoramic view.

In the Mexican exhibit, there was a sign which read: "Try the Mexican drinks." One of the male visitors to the exhibit tried one of the drinks, and he was assured by the vendor that there was no wine in the drink. The vendor told him that the drink was some sort of lemonade. The visitor drank two-thirds of the glass, but the peculiar taste of clear liquid did not agree with the man's palate. The visitor started off without paying, and when he was reminded by a companion that he must leave a nickel, the visitor became "politely indignant."[88] The visitor paid the bill. Half an hour later, the visitor was sitting on a bench in front of the roller coaster and looking at the stand where a man was selling Michigan apple cider, but visitor called the cider "Midgigan awble siger." The visitor hiccupped: "I muz-hic-try all drinksh, but not thi sevening. 'Smother eve-hic-ning. Mexicanish lem'nade don't-hic-'gree with me."[89] The visitor got up and headed for the Art Gallery and called the attention of a reporter to the artistic painting of a small dog, which was lying in a corner of the vestibule. Unfortunately the dog was real, and when the man came too close to the animal, the dog growled and walked away. The visitor then apologized, saying that the strong drink made him disturb the painting of the dog.[90]

One of the exhibits at the exposition belonged to George Payne, who manufactured cordage and twine. The only other competitor with Kentucky's hemp was Missouri. The exhibit displayed Kentucky hemp, packing and all other classes of goods in his line, all handmade. In the display, there was a bale of double-dressed Kentucky hemp; one bale of imported sea grass; and two bales of jute, imported from east India. Jute was commonly made into bagging.

On August 22, the exposition decided to have a People's Day, in which they lowered the admission fee to twenty-five cents. In 1884, the admission was fifty cents, but it was lowered to twenty-five cents on Mondays and Saturdays. More season tickets were sold in one week than what was sold in four weeks the previous year. The exposition originally had a contract with Detweiler and Street for the fireworks display, but the public found his shows disappointing, so the exposition board brought back Paine, from England.

In the Machinery Hall, located near the southwest corner of the building, a miniature house was enclosed by a picket fence, with plants and flowers in the yard. The house was for the Institute for the Education of Feeble Minded Children, which was located outside of Frankfort, Kentucky. The institute taught common school education but also various trades and industries, such as gardening, shoemaking, carpentry, broom making, upholstery for boys and laundry work and hand and machine sewing for girls. The building and its contents were made by the inmates from the institution.

In the French exhibit, an exact reproduction of the table used by the king of Bohemia was on display. The French exhibit also had their beautiful handcrafted porcelain dolls. The Pioneer Silk Company donated the first twenty yards of ribbon, which was woven by workers inside the exposition. The ribbon was donated to the permanent Exposition Room. The hay press at the exposition turned out compact little bales that visitors could take home as a souvenir. Also in the exposition, the smallest engine ever made was on display; it was made from a single five-cent piece and ran by steam or wind power. There was a Russian exhibit, and the Italian exhibit had a number of character figures in terra cotta. In one of the exhibits, they were giving away free biscuits.

The exposition had a railroad exhibit put on by the Baltimore & Ohio Railroad, which linked the Atlantic seaboard with the Ohio River. The company owned not only the railway but also the telegraph service, express business, sleeping cars, hotels and summer resorts. The company started in 1828. The first cornerstone of the railway company's building, which was laid by Charles Carroll, the last survivor of the signers of the Declaration of Independence, was on display at the exposition. The spade, hammer and trowel, which were burnished, polished and used at the cornerstone laying ceremony, were on exhibit at the exposition. A section of the original track was also displayed. The B&O also displayed primitive passenger coaches and a model of a locomotive used a half century before the exposition. There was also a model of the first telegraph instrument used to transmit the message "What hath God wrought?" The Baltimore & Ohio was the first railroad to carry passengers and the first to introduce steam locomotive engines. The exhibit had several large pictures of scenes along the route, with some of the photographs being the largest ones ever taken. Mr. J.G. Pangborn, assistant general passenger agent of the Baltimore & Ohio Railroad, helped design the display. The exhibit was transferred from New Orleans to the Southern Exposition.

The exposition added a skating rink, which cost fifteen cents to enter. One of the most admired foreign exhibits at the exposition was that of the Florentine vases, near the fountain. They were four feet high and covered with flowers and shrubs, and on either side, there were dragons holding onto the edges with their teeth.

On August 28, during the nightly fireworks display, the fixed pieces were large and beautiful with showers of gold. During the fireworks

An 1885 souvenir ice cream soda mug from the Southern Exposition. Ice cream sodas were introduced to Louisville residents for the first time at the Southern Exposition. *Courtesy of the author.*

A view of the back of the ice cream soda mug from the 1885 Southern Exposition. The advertisement was for an M.J. Tapp. *Courtesy of the author.*

display, there were trees of gold, portraits made of fireworks, a shell that burst and spread a canopy of green stars over the entire eight acres of the enclosed ampitheater and a huge device, with a message, saying, "Louisville Welcomes Our Foreign Exhibitors." There were also mechanical devices that were illuminated with fireworks. The fireworks display ended with a flight of five hundred rockets that created a bouquet of color in the air.[91]

With so many visitors to the exposition, the hotels' capacities were pushed to their maximum. Many displays in the hotel windows read: "Standing room only." At Alexander's hotel, every room was full, and many guests slept on cots. By October 25, 1885, within a ten-week period, over 400,000 people had attended the Southern Exposition.[92] It was a complete success, and at the end of the run, the Exposition Board decided to have another show in 1886.

Chapter 6
Dinosaurs Come to the Exposition

On August 28, 1886, the Southern Exposition was ready for another season. Major Wright and his crew worked on the new exhibits and decorated the building. The northern section of the building added the Ward collection of minerals and specimens of natural history; another change was made to the large lighted fountain. The exposition committee replaced the fountain with a replica of a lighthouse, complete with a beacon light and a rock base surrounded with water. A Japanese village also was added to the exposition. One of the biggest changes was the loss of the use of Central Park, since the exposition was denied further use of it. The Exposition Committee paid the owners of Central Park $2,000 for eight weeks. The cost of lighting the park, maintenance and guards was between $1,500 and $2,000. The Art Gallery in the park cost $5,000 to build. The directors of the exposition decided to save their money by relocating the Art Gallery to the exposition building.

On opening day, businesses closed at noon. There was a parade, just like in years past. The police department, fire department and Louisville Legion formed at Seventh and Market Streets and moved out at 2:00 p.m., with the route following up Market to Third to the exposition. The policemen were dressed in their new uniforms, wearing white gloves, and carried rosewood clubs. Chief John Whallen rode at the head of the column, along with the Louisville Legion band, under the command

The lighthouse at the Southern Exposition. *Courtesy of the* Louisville Courier-Journal.

of Drum Major Roberts. The fire department display included twelve engines, two hook and ladder companies and the supply wagons; the engines and horses were decorated. Fire captain Ben F. Bache rode on horseback at the head of the column, wearing a fireman's hat and a white flannel shirt. The firemen wore red hats, blue shirts with silver buttons and a button-hole bouquet in his badge. The three hundred men of the Louisville Legion, making six companies, marched in the parade, with the drum corps leading the way, followed by Major W. H. Coen, who was in command, and assisted by Major James Kelly. The next groups followed: Battery A, under Captain Huhlein; Company F, under Captain H. C. Grinstead; Company B, under Lieutenant W.T. Hunt; Company A, under Captain E. McPherson; Company D, under Captain D.W. Gray; and Company C, under Captain G.E. Bly.

Behind them came a carriage containing William Campbell Preston Breckinridge and several gentlemen.

When the parade arrived at the exposition, the guns of the Louisville Legion battery unlimbered, and a salute of fifteen guns was fired. After the salute, the ranks broke up, and Mr. Breckinridge, arm in arm with Dr. George W. Griffiths, marched into the exposition, followed by Governor R.W. Knott, Senator James Beck, Richard W. Tate, Arthur Carey, W.H. Wathen, Carey Blackburn, Thomas Freely, Merriwether Lewis Clark Jr., W.R. Belnap, Jesse Middleton, Wiley Rogers, Cushman Quarrier, Bennett Young, J.M. Wright, Captain Gifford, W.J. Davis, Harry Weissinger, C.H. Pettit, John E. Green, Judge Bruce, James C. Gilbert, F.C. Leber, T.P. Satterwhite and C.E. Craik. Congressman Breckinridge marched through a line of spectators into the building and took his seat, and the other members of the committee took their seats on the stage of the Music Hall. Major J.M. Wright stepped forward and announced the opening ceremonies. The Reverend C.E. Craik of the Christ Church Cathedral gave a prayer, after which Major Wright introduced Colonel W.C.P. Breckinridge. Colonel Breckinridge came from one of the most prominent political families in Kentucky. His grandfather served as U.S. senator, was the first cabinet-level minister from west of the Appalachians and introduced the Kentucky Resolutions of 1798. His father, Robert, left politics for the ministry and became moderator of the Presbyterian General Assembly. His cousin was John C. Breckinridge, who was a senator, vice president of the United States and, during the Civil War, Confederate general of the Kentucky Orphan Brigade and Confederate secretary of war. During the Civil War, William Breckinridge joined the Confederate Ninth Kentucky Cavalry and was elected major. Later, the Confederate government promoted Breckinridge to colonel of the cavalry. The Ninth Kentucky Cavalry rode with General John Hunt Morgan and participated in Morgan's "Christmas Raid" of 1862, the Battle of Lookout Mountain, Missionary Ridge, Tunnel Hill, the Atlanta Campaign, the March to the Sea Campaign and the Battle of Bentonville, North Carolina. The regiment escorted Confederate president Jefferson Davis and his cabinet to Charlotte, North Carolina, on April 18, 1865. On May 10, 1865, William Breckinridge and the Ninth Kentucky Cavalry rode to Washington, Georgia, and surrendered.[93]

After the war, William Breckinridge entered politics and married the granddaughter of Henry Clay, the Great Compromiser. When she died, he married a granddaughter of a former Kentucky governor. He was the father of five children. Breckinridge was known for his oratory skills and speeches, for which he was nicknamed "the silver tongued orator from Kentucky." People came from all around Kentucky to listen to his speeches on diverse topics, such as religion, imperialism, race relations, politics and morals. To keep his image as a man of morals, he did not drink, smoke, play cards or bet.[94]

Breckinridge served for five terms as a member of the U.S. House of Representatives. At the Southern Exposition, Breckinridge was at his political high. Long after the exposition in 1893, Breckinridge's career came to halt. A woman named Madeline Pollard petitioned the court that she be given $50,000 because Breckinridge promised to marry her but broke the contract. On April 1, 1884, Pollard filed another petition that stated when she was seventeen, Breckinridge seduced her and she claimed that Breckinridge "completed his seduction of her." She claimed that, since that time, she not only had been his mistress, but that she had also given birth to two of his sons. In 1893, after Breckinridge's wife died, he promised to marry her, but he married another woman. Madeline sued for breach of contract. Breckinridge fought the lawsuit, but the court found him guilty and ordered him to pay $15,000. His scandal made national press, and when he ran for election, the race literally divided families, churches and neighborhoods. He lost the election by only 255 votes. Breckinridge never returned to politics.[95]

After his introduction, Colonel Breckinridge arose and gave his speech. In his speech, he welcomed the public to the Southern Exposition. He expressed that, like the general public, he was at the exposition for pleasure and rest. He pointed out that it was a "victory of labor, the trophies of sweat-sweat of the brow, sweat of the brain and of the heart."[96] He told the public that they should bring their children to the exposition the same as "the fathers of Israel brought their children to the Ark of the covenant, when it was brought out from the holy of holies for the glory of God."[97] He spoke of how Louisville, only one hundred years before, only existed in men's dreams, yet now the railroad connected the city to distant areas. Breckinridge received applause from the public when he said:

Centuries ago the greatest of Grecian statesmen and the second of Grecian orators in eulogizing the dead did not speak of the Athens of palaces, but of a country where the laws were wise, justice was all pervading, patriotism rewarded. He spoke of a city men might well love to build and for which they might well love to die. It is in this aspect that our county is dear to my heart. 'Tis for her free institutions that I love her, her boundless opportunities, her old fashioned faith in God and her ceaseless love for man.

Breckinridge stated that the exposition expressed those qualities. He said that when the visitor walked through the exposition, they were taught that it is not the work they do that dignifies, but it is how they do it.

It is not the characteristic of the work, but the mode in which it is done. Step by step, we see here what we would see as we walk through the corridors of nature could we recognize in the rustling forest, the painted petal of the flower, the rush of the storm-in all that fills the heart with love or awe-the hand of one man. As that is the handiwork of God, so this is the apotheosis of man.[98]

To Breckinridge, all labor was noble and honorable. He concluded his speech, stating that before the machines are turned on in the exposition, that the children of Kentucky and Louisville be trained and equipped to be leaders. He stated: "In the light of the new dawn we see evidences in the streets of the East of the glories it is given to you to win. God grant that you take advantage of the opportunity."[99] After his speech, Senator James B. Beck arose and spoke briefly. Senator Beck was born on February 13, 1822, in Dumfriesshire, Scotland. In 1838, Beck immigrated to America and settled in Wyoming County, New York. In 1843, he moved to Lexington, Kentucky, and graduated from Transylvania University. After being admitted to the Kentucky bar, he practiced law in Lexington. Before the Civil War broke out, he set up a law practice with John C. Breckinridge, who was a Confederate general. After the war, Beck was elected to the United States House of Representatives, serving Kentucky's Seventh District from 1867 to 1875. In 1877, he was elected the United States Senate and served until 1890.[100] During his speech,

Beck appreciated the importance of the exposition. He said that it was the inspiration for the possibility of things.

After Senator Beck's speech, Walter Damrosch and his orchestra of sixty musicians played the first concert of the season. He started off playing Faust's "Fantasie" and Liszt's "Rhapsody No. 14."

The Art Gallery surpassed the collections of 1884 and 1885. The center of the large room was decorated with a little garden of palms and tropical plants. According to the *Louisville Courier-Journal*, the gallery also surpassed any of the other public exhibitions of the season, whether in New York or elsewhere. There were 442 paintings in the collection. The painting that received the most attention from visitors was *The Strike*, by Robert Koehler. Also on display were *The Gossips*, by Carl Marr; *The French Revolution*, by Philippoteaux; Swain Gifford's *Seaweed Gatherer*; Childe Hassam's *Dusk*; Henry Poore's *Close of a City Day*; Francis Millet's *Flower Girl*; Levi Ruggles Church's *Pegasus Captured*; William Sontag's *Mount Washington*; and John Henry Dolph's *Kittens*. There were also landscapes by George Inness, Alexander Wyant, Bolton Jones, Deway, Tyron and Dubois Fenelon Hasbrouck. Many of the paintings were for sale, except those on loan by the Buffalo Fine Arts Academy and two other patrons.

As for the fireworks display, the Southern Exposition changed the theme from the "Storming of the Bastille" to "The Last Days of Pompeii," and showed the pyrotechnics at the new grounds south of the exposition building. There was a spacious forum, and on three sides rose the buildings of Pompeii, and behind the towers, the threatening summit of Vesuvius. In front spread the waters of a real lake, extending the full length of the open spaces. The building and the mountain were artistically arranged, and the painters gave the paper-covered framework an appearance of the originals. The structure at one end of the lake was supposed to be the temple of Jupiter. Behind the lake and fronting the forum were the seats for the spectators.[101]

The opening scene showed the gathering of the people in the forum to witness the athletic exercises of the Romans. There was the Roman senator in his toga, the flower girl, the beggar and the priests; flower-decked barges that floated across the lake; and Roman centurions in their uniforms. As the gymnasts and priests, who were chanting "Take me back to the Sweet Sunny South," left the forum and the procession left the stage, Mount Vesuvius erupted, and flames, rockets and smoke poured out from the crater. The crash of falling buildings added to the pyrotechnic effect. After the eruption, Paine's fireworks display took over and entertained the spectators.[102]

Another new addition to the exposition was Ward's Natural Science collection, which contained restorations of the skeletons of the Siberian mammoth, which came from the Royal Museum of Stuttgart, Germany. There were also skeletons of the megatherium; the Himalayan mammoth; the cryptodon, from the Argentine Republic; and the deinotherium, from the valley of the Rhine. In the center of the south wall, a huge hanging plesiosaurus was flanked by an ichthyosaurus and a smaller plesiosaurus and completely surrounded by other animals of the earlier times. Near the dinosaurs were copies in clay of all the most noted geological specimens from European museums, along with hundreds of specimens of minerals and copies of brass of all the noted gold nuggets of the world; there was also Mexican onyx called tecali. A zoological collection contained mounted specimens of nearly all known rare mammals and birds. A group of orangutans fed on their native durion fruit, and there was a skeleton of a Japanese crab, which was nine feet from tip to tip.

A sketch of the dinosaur display at the Southern Exposition. Notice the Swiss chalet in the background. *Courtesy of the* Louisville Courier-Journal.

Another addition to the exposition was the Japanese display, which contained a number of Japanese houses lit with lanterns. The display was built by Sarto, a Japanese carpenter. Inside the houses, Japanese people sat among displays of their native country's industry.

One of the new attractions to the exposition was the D.H. Baldwin & Company exhibit. The Steinway Cabinet Grand Piano arrived at the exposition with engraved panels. Pony and Parlor Grand Piano of Steinway and Decker Brothers had their latest models. Decker Brothers had a new style piano with eighteen ebony engraved and carved keys, which they also offered in a curled walnut wood. Haines Brothers and Fischer offered upright pianos. All the pianos on display were for sale.

W.H. McKnight & Company, which was located in the center aisle, opposite the Fourth Street entrance, displayed the latest novelties in Wilton, moquette, velvet, Brussels and tapestry carpets; velour, chenille, shela, madras and lace curtains; rugs; and mats.

Chase & Sanborn was the largest importer of coffee in the United States. Mr. Conde Tabb, manager of the southwestern division department, located on 424 West Main Street, helped to put together the display. His exhibit served tiny cups of Java coffee and also their C&S brand of Java and mocha, with pure cream and lump sugar.

Scanlan & Company had two displays measuring twenty by thirty feet, one on each side of the Art Gallery. The ceilings and walls were artistically finished, and the floor was Brussels carpet. They sold brass, marbleized iron and slate mantels.

The Dow Wire Works Company was Louisville's leading manufacturer, and for the exposition, they made comfortable wire chairs. Bridgeford & Company, located in the center aisle, just to the west of the entrance to the Art Gallery and Music Hall, had a raised platform covering thirty-five feet by sixty feet. The floor was covered in Brussels carpet, and it had a pagoda-shaped roof. There were arches with various colored lights that ran down the whole length of the aisle. The company sold stoves and ranges; one of their stoves was the open-faced Orient. Also present in the exhibit were the wholesale agents for the Preston Stove Works of New York and Boston, the Michigan Stove Works of Chicago and Detroit, the Fuller & Warre Company of Cleveland, Ohio, and the Buck's Stove and Range Company of St. Louis. There was the Royal American cookstove, which was mounted entirely in nickel and gold; the Radiant Home baseburner, which was nickel plated; the Economist; the American; and hotel ranges. They also displayed heating furnaces.

R.N. Ewall & Company, located midway of the southeast side of the building, sold the Bull of the Woods and other famous brands of cigars. They set up a regular cigar factory complete with every detail. They had sixty people working day and night making cigars. The display space was twenty-four feet by sixty feet, and a three-sided panel surrounded a cigar makers table. In the center of the exhibit was a column of cigar boxes, surmounted by the company's sign and a life-size painting of a bull. The public could see the entire process of the manufacture of cigars, from the tobacco on the leaf to the finished product, and boxed cigars ready for the market. People could also examine samples and get a fresh cigar.

One of the highlights of the exhibition was Paul Philippoteaux's *The Battle of Gettysburg* cyclorama. In 1883, Phillippoteaux painted *Picket's Charge*, which was the climax of the Confederate attack on Union forces at Gettysburg, Pennsylvania, on July 3, 1863. He painted four different versions; which version was at the exposition is unknown. The painting measured 27 feet by 359 feet. The cyclorama enhanced the painting with trees, grasses, fences and life-sized figures. The result was a three-dimensional effect that surrounded the viewers, who stood on a central platform that literally placed the viewer in the center of the historic event. When the cyclorama opened in 1883 in Chicago for the first time, the painting was complete with a three-dimensional earthen foreground littered with the relics of battle, stone walls, shattered trees and broken fences.[103] On the first day of public viewing at the exposition, over five hundred visitors came to see the cyclorama.

On September 1 and 2, 1886, the exposition invited all Kentucky growers of fruit to compete for prizes. A grand display of apples, pears, peaches and grapes were placed on tables. A show of honey was also allowed for competition. Evaporated fruit and wine and cider were also judged. Colonel Bennett Young, Thomas Kennedy and I.B. Nall managed the competition.

Chapter 7
The End of the Show

Amazingly, there were no opening ceremonies, parades or speeches. One of the additions to the 1887 exposition was a Shetland pony track under the gallery in the southeast section. The track was three hundred feet long with a return of the same length. Each track was fifteen feet wide. Bells from Boston arrived, and they were located at the south end of the Kentucky Machinery Company. The bells would be rung every half an hour before closing. Eichorn's band arrived at the exposition, replacing Damrosch. Professor Turk entertained children with his exhibitions of sleight of hand and juggling. He also included a show of marionettes. The southern end of the building was set aside for bicycle riding and roller-skating. A string band provided the music.

The Japanese Troupe gave a matinee in the Music Hall, and Eichorn's band was required to act as orchestra, since there was no regular afternoon concert. From the newly remodeled bandstand, Professor Eichorn played a few selections before the Japanese Troupe came on stage; he didn't have an officially prepared program. His band included twenty-one pieces, and only the latest music or classical compositions would be played. During the afternoon promenade concerts, which lasted from 2:00 p.m. to 6:00 p.m., Professor Eichorn's men wore their military uniforms; when they provided music for the theatrical attractions, they wore their dress suits.[104]

The Japanese Troupe opened the exposition, and they were one of the strongest attractions presented in New York. The program included acrobats, balancers, top spinners, dancers and equilibrists. W.H. Alexander, who was the manager of the troupe, introduced them in their royal garments. Soto Kichi, who performed bending, somersaulting and acrobatic exercises, performed first. Those following were: Suna Kichi, a great Japanese funambulist, with his rope act; Tenara Jisaka, the top spinner; Miss Hannah performed feats and evolutions using rice barrels, tubs and other items; and Sunetaro Unakiahi underwent conjuring and prestidigitation. There were pyramid contortions; the great juggler of the Mikado, Watanabe and Masakichi; and Sunetaro and Lunakichi balanced mammoth screens in their act. The troupe also performed Japanese national dances, with singing and music.

When the visitor entered the middle section of the exposition, they were greeted by two large pyramids with a smaller one in between them. The large pyramid on the right was from New York and displayed preparations made by a drug house. In the neighboring section, the visitor saw retail druggists who made certain preparations. In other parts of the building, a visitor could see Indianapolis and other places showing off their medicines, extracts and preparations. The smaller pyramid at the entrance displayed the goods of a tailoring merchant. The great clothing houses had displays elsewhere. The pyramid on the left was from Louisville. There was a carpet and curtain pavilion, arranged with cases of ladies' goods and long lines of decoration, which ran for six hundred feet across the middle section.

Mr. R.T. McDonald, manager of the Fort Wayne Jenney Electric Light Company, arrived at the exposition to install new wires and lights, including new engines providing the power for the lights. Unfortunately, one night a pump broke down in the boiler house and the steam ran low, causing the lights to dim.[105] But overall, most people complimented the new lights when they did work.

One of the popular features of the 1887 exposition was the admission of a party of foreigners who spoke an unknown language and sold balloons and a device consisting of a slender stick and a dangling beetle at the end. Some of the Wild West children bought the devices. The children would swing the bug past the face of a "serious lady," who became frightened at the bug.

Professor Herrmann, the famous magician, arrived in Louisville. His vanishing lady trick was said to be one of the best of his acts. Madame Herrmann was seated in full sight of the audience on a chair that was on top of an open newspaper. Herrmann covered her with a piece of Indian silk so that her outline could be distinguished. He then extended the silk so that the outline disappeared and then drew away the silk. The chair and newspaper remained, but Madame Herrmann had disappeared.

George Brown brought his exhibit from Galesburg, Illinois, and it was located in the machinery department. Other exhibitors were the Stuber Brothers' photograph display, the Mammoth Clothing House and the Wilson & Rankins minstrel show. The Astoria Veneer Company built a display of its wood, but the company also introduced a quartet of musicians from among its own employees. The employees explained their work and drew attention to their exhibit with their own music.

The exposition booked the Bijou Opera Company of New York. A regular Exposition Opera Festival was given, and sixteen performances were held, at which eight operas were performed. On September 12, the first opera performed the *Mikado*, followed by *Victor*, *Merry War*, *Chimes of Normandy*, *Billie Taylor*, *Pinafore*, *Olivette* and *Robert Macaire*. The Bijou Opera Company had thirty-five artists. The scenery and stage effects added to the performances. Two matinees were performed each week, one on Thursday and the other on Saturday. The scenery—the largest in the United States—for the different operas was purchased from a large lot from New York. The exposition stage was refitted in 1887 to accommodate the scenery of the National Opera Company, which most theaters in the United States could not. There were fourteen hours of continuous entertainment.

The fireworks display was also new in 1887. "The Burning of Moscow" and the picture of Judge Toney were the highlights of the pyrotechnic show. Mr. Walker, the florist, exhibited his night-blooming cereus. The plant only blooms once a year.

When October arrived, the Southern Exposition board decided not to continue the show for another year; it had run its course. The exposition had an amazing run that exposed Louisville residents to products they never dreamed of buying or using. They learned about foreign cultures and food; roller coasters, roller skating, dinosaurs, electric railways, light bulbs, bicycle tracks, opera and orchestras; and they also witnessed some of the most outstanding art collections in the United States. Many of these traditions still carry into Louisville's present. Louisville still has its international festival on the waterfront and the outstanding J.B. Speed Art Gallery. The city also has a love for the arts, with the Actors Theater and the Kentucky Center for the Arts. In Central Park, Louisville still carries on the tradition of Shakespeare in the Park. The city has continued to be a mixture of northern industry and southern hospitality. One needs to look no further than UPS, Ford, GE, YUM, United Distillers and many other industries to see that Louisville has maintained the strive for progress. The huge Kentucky Derby Festival also signifies the open southern hospitality that Louisville residents offer to the world.

Chapter 8

The Southern Exposition Legacy

The Southern Exposition served as a catalyst for development in the surrounding area. In 1885, 260 homes valued at an average cost of $6,150, or $1.6 million today, were constructed between Kentucky and Magnolia Streets. After the Southern Exposition closed its doors in 1887, William Slaughter, president of the Victoria Land Company, bought the vacated property. That same year, the city began to collect over $10 million worth in construction contracts. The most popular Victorian-style houses built were the Queen Anne and the Richardsonian Romanesque. On March 1887, the *Courier-Journal* declared Louisville the "New Gotham" and hailed that the city had the most beautiful homes. That year, Louisville had ninety-four miles of street railways; 19 million people rode them. By 1890, Louisville had 161,129 residents, making the city twentieth in urban size in the United States. The city had grown to a stable manufacturing and commercial base: it became the world's largest tobacco market; by the 1890s Louisville had nineteen distilleries; and the city was also the largest producer of cast iron pipe, made by Dennis Long & Company, and the world's largest producer of plows, made by Avery & Company. Louisville also became the largest producers of jean cloth, producing eight million yards every year. The city also had sixteen tanneries with $2.5 million in sales annually. Louisville also expanded its woodworking industry and meatpacking houses.[106] Louisville lived up

Left: A close-up view of the Saint James Court fountain, which stands on the site of the Southern Exposition. *Courtesy of the author.*

Below: The courtyard of Saint James Court, which stands on the Southern Exposition grounds. *Courtesy of the author.*

One of the beautiful homes in Saint James Court. *Courtesy of the author.*

The Conrad-Caldwell House, which stands on the front entrance to Saint James Court. It was previously the front entrance to the Southern Exposition. *Courtesy of the author.*

The Southern Exposition monument, located to the front entrance to Saint James Court. It was previously the front entrance to the Southern Exposition. *Courtesy of the author.*

to the city's motto: The City of Progress. In 1890, the exposition site was transformed into the Saint James Court and Belgravia development, which still stands today as a testament to the Southern Exposition's ideals of commerce and progress, southern hospitality and northern ingenuity.

Notes

1. The History of Expositions and Fairs in the United States and Louisville

1. *Louisville Courier-Journal*, August 1, 1883.
2. Ibid.
3. Ibid.
4. Ibid.
5. Ibid.
6. Ibid.
7. Ibid.

2. The Idea and Building of the Southern Exposition

8. *New York Herald*, July 31, 1883.
9. Kleber, et al., *The Encyclopedia of Louisville*, 925.
10. Ibid.
11. Ibid.
12. Ibid.

13. Ibid.
14. *Louisville Courier-Journal*, August 1, 1883.
15. "Southern Exposition," 38–39.
16. Kleber, et al., *The Encyclopedia of Louisville*, 258.
17. *Louisville Courier-Journal*, August 2, 1883.
18. Ibid.
19. Ibid.
20. Ibid.
21. Ibid.

3. The Opening of the Southern Exposition

22. *Louisville Courier-Journal*, August 2, 1883.
23. Ibid.
24. Ibid.
25. Ibid.
26. Kleber, et al., *The Encyclopedia of Louisville*, 557.
27. Ibid.
28. Ibid.
29. Ibid., 163–64.
30. *Louisville Courier-Journal*, August 2, 1883.
31. Ibid.
32. Ibid.
33. ibid.
34. ibid.
35. Kramer, *Old Louisville*, 84–85.
36. *Louisville Courier-Journal*, August 2, 1882.
37. *Louisville Courier-Journal*, August 16, 1884.

4. The Southern Exposition Puts on a Military Show

38. Kinchen, *General Bennett H. Young*, 15–21.
39. Kleber, et al., *The Encyclopedia of Louisville*, 962–62.

40. Kleber, et al., *The Encyclopedia of Louisville*, 198–99; Holmberg, "The Clark Family."
41. Patrick Sarsfield Gilmore.
42. *Louisville Courier-Journal*, August 15, 1884.
43. Ibid.
44. *Louisville Courier-Journal*, August 17, 1884.
45. Ibid.
46. Ibid.
47. Kleber, *The Kentucky Encyclopedia*, 522.
48. *Louisville Courier-Journal*, August 16, 1884.
49. Jacobson, "Eminent Coronet Virtuosi," 58–62.
50. *Louisville Courier-Journal*, August 17, 1884.
51. Ibid.
52. *Louisville Courier Journal*, August 26, 1884.
53. Ibid.
54. Ibid.
55. Ibid.
56. Ibid.
57. *Louisville Courier Journal*, August 26, 1884.
58. *Louisville Courier Journal*, August 31, 1884.
59. Ibid.
60. Ibid.
61. *Louisville Courier Journal*, August 26, 1884.
62. *Louisville Courier-Journal*, August 21, 1884.
63. Ibid.
64. Ibid.
65. Barbara Zingman, "Loaded Guns and Loaded Soldiers," *Louisville Times*, May 12, 1959.
66. *The Louisville Courier Journal*, August 26, 1884
67. Ibid.
68. Ibid.
69. *Louisville Courier Journal*, August 26, 1884.
70. *Louisville Courier Journal*, August 27, 1884.
71. Ibid.
72. Ibid.
73. Ibid.

74. *Louisville Courier Journal*, August 29, 1884.
75. Ibid.
76. *Louisville Courier Journal*, August 31, 1884.
77. Ibid.
78. Ibid.

5. The Southern Exposition Becomes a World's Fair

79. *Louisville Courier Journal*, August 15, 1885.
80. Ibid.
81. *Louisville Courier Journal*, August 15, 1885.
82. Kleber, et al., *The Encyclopedia of Louisville*, 129–30.
83. *Louisville Courier Journal*, August 16, 1885.
84. Ibid.
85. *Louisville Courier Journal*, August 15, 1885.
86. Performing Arts Encyclopedia.
87. *Louisville Courier Journal*, August 16, 1885.
88. *Louisville Courier-Journal*, August 27, 1885.
89. Ibid.
90. Ibid.
91. *Louisville Courier-Journal*, August 28, 1885.
92. *New York Times*, October 25, 1885.

6. Dinosaurs Come to the Exposition

93. Bryan Bush, *The Civil War Battles of the Western Theater*, (Turner Publishing, Paducah, Kentucky, 1998, reprint 2000), 168–69.
94. Ibid.
95. Bush, *The Civil War Battles*, 169–70.
96. *Louisville Courier-Journal*, August 29, 1886.
97. Ibid.
98. Ibid.
99. Ibid.

100. Biographical Directory of the United States Congress.
101. *Louisville Courier-Journal*, August 29, 1886.
102. Ibid.
103. Gettysburg National Military Park.

7. The End of the Show

104. *Louisville Courier Journal*, August 28, 1887.
105. Ibid.

8. The Southern Exposition Legacy

106. Yater, *Two Hundred Years*, 122–23.

Sources

Biographical Directory of the United States Congress. http://www.bioguide.congress.gov.

Bush, Bryan. *The Civil War Battles of the Western Theater*. Paducah, KY: Turner Publishing, 1998. Reprint, 2000.

Gettysburg National Military Park. U.S. National Park Service, http://www.nps.gov/gett/historyculture/gettysburg-cyclorama.htm.

Kinchen, Oscar A. *General Bennett Young: Confederate Raider and a Man of Many Adventures*. West Hanover, MA: Christopher Publishing House, 1981.

Kleber, John, editor in chief; Mary J. Kinsman, managing editor; Thomas Clark, Clyde Crews and George Yater, associate editors. *The Encyclopedia of Louisville*. Lexington: University of Kentucky Press, 2001.

Kleber, John, ed., *The Kentucky Encyclopedia*. Lexington: University of Kentucky Press, n.d.

Kramer, Carl E. *Old Louisville: A Changing View*. Louisville, KY: Old Louisville Neighborhood Council, Inc., 1982.

Patrick Sarsfield Gilmore. Boston Irish Tourism Association, http://www.psgilmore-society.org.

Performing Arts Encyclopedia. Library of Congress, http://www.libraryofcongress.gov.

Yater, George. *Two Hundred Years at the Falls of the Ohio: A History of Louisville and Jefferson County*. Louisville, KY: Heritage Corporation, 1979.

ARTICLES

Holmberg, James. "The Clark Family and the Kentucky Derby," *Filson Historical Quarterly* 4, no. 1.

Jacobson, Sam. "Eminent Coronet Virtuosi, Past and Present," *Music: A Monthly Magazine* 15 (1890).

"Southern Exposition, 1883." *Kentucky Explorer* 11, no. 2 (June 1996).

NEWSPAPERS

Harpers Weekly
Jefferson County Gazette
Louisville Courier-Journal
Louisville Times
New York Herald
New York Times

Index

About the Author

Bryan Bush was born in 1966 in Louisville, Kentucky, and has been a native of that city ever since. He graduated with honors from Murray State University with a degree in history and psychology and received his master's degree in 2005 from the University of Louisville.

Bryan has always had a passion for history, especially the Civil War. He has been a member of many different Civil War historical preservation societies; consulted for movie companies and other authors; coordinated with other museums on displays of various museum articles and artifacts; written for magazines, such as *Kentucky Civil War Magazine*, *North/South Trader* and *Back Home in Kentucky*; and worked for many different historical sites. He has always fought hard to maintain and preserve Civil War history in the western theater. In 1999, Bryan published his first work, *The Civil War Battles of the Western Theater*, which was given good reviews by *North/South Magazine* and *Kentucky Monthly*. *Kentucky Monthly* said Bryan Bush's *The Civil War Battles of the Western*

Theater "has with his first book created a needed addition to any serious Civil War library." Since then, Mr. Bush has had published *Terry's Texas Rangers: The 8th Texas Cavalry*, *My Dearest Mollie: The Civil War Letters of Brig. Gen. Daniel F. Griffin, 38th Indiana Volunteer Infantry* and *Lloyd Tilghman: Confederate General in the Western Theater*. He was also a contributor to *Kentucky's Civil War*, *Louisville During the Civil War: A History and Guide*, *Lincoln and the Speeds: An Enduring and Devoted Friendship*, *Butcher Burbridge: Union General Stephen Gano Burbridge and His Reign of Terror over Kentucky* and *Haunted Battlefields of the South*. Bryan Bush has been a Civil War reenactor for fourteen years, portraying an artillerist. For five years, Bryan was on the board of directors and curator for the Old Bardstown Civil War Museum and Village: The Battles of the Western Theater Museum in Bardstown, Kentucky.